Yale Library Studies
LIBRARY ARCHITECTURE AT YALE

2009

Yale University Library · New Haven

DISTRIBUTED BY
Yale University Press · New Haven and London

ABOUT THE SERIES

Yale Library Studies succeeds the *Yale University Library Gazette*, which was published in eighty-two volumes from 1926 to 2008 and edited by a series of distinguished scholar-librarians, including Donald C. Gallup, Stephen Parks, and Patricia C. Willis.

Each volume of Yale Library Studies, which will be published annually, will explore a different theme and will contain articles by Yale faculty, library staff, experts in that particular field, and invited authors. The inaugural volume, *Library Architecture at Yale,* will be followed by ones exploring the collections and collectors who built them and teaching and learning with collections.

EDITED BY
Geoffrey Little

PUBLISHED BY
Yale University Library
P.O. Box 208240
New Haven, Connecticut 06520-8240
www.library.yale.edu

DISTRIBUTED BY
Yale University Press
P.O. Box 209040
New Haven, Connecticut 06520-9040
www.yalebooks.com

Designed by Katy Homans
Copy edited by Joyce Ippolito
Text set in Yale, designed by Matthew Carter
Printed by GHP, West Haven, Connecticut,
under the supervision of John S. Robinson

Copyright 2009 by Yale University.

Every effort has been made to credit artists and sources;
if there are any errors or omissions, please contact the Editor.

ISBN 978-0-300-16477-0
A catalog record is available from Yale University Library

cover: *Design for a University Library* by Bertram Grosvenor Goodhue, 1924.
From *Bertram Grosvenor Goodhue: Architect and Master of Many Arts*
(New York: American Institute of Architects, 1925). Used with permission.
Elevation drawing of the Beinecke Library by Gordon Bunshaft, 1963.
Photographs of the Beinecke Rare Book and Manuscript Library, Yale University, 1961–1963.
Manuscripts and Archives, Yale University Library.

page 4: *Bibliotheca for Yale* by Alexander Jackson Davis (1803–1892).
Pen and ink with watercolor wash, 1830.
Beinecke Rare Book and Manuscript Library, Yale University.

Contents

Introduction
ALICE PROCHASKA
5

Library Architecture at Yale
ROBERT A.M. STERN
13

Crossing Wall
MARJORIE G. WYNNE
67

Reconstituting the Legacy
CHARLES GWATHMEY
73

The Lewis Walpole Library Puzzle
MARK SIMON
85

Twice Borrowed: The Arches and Pinnacles of Strawberry Hill
MARGARET K. POWELL
97

Cathedral, Cloister, Crypt: Bass and the Evolution of the Yale Library
ARIC LASHER
103

Rethinking Library Spaces
DANUTA A. NITECKI
131

The Architectural Archives at Yale University Library
LAURA TATUM
137

Contributors
150

Yale University Library Administration
153

BIBLIOTHECA FOR YALE, DONE IN 1830 BY A.J.D.

ALICE PROCHASKA

Introduction

Yale Library Studies is a new publication by the Yale University Library, intended to replace the former *Yale University Library Gazette*, the journal produced for many years for members of the Yale Library Associates and other subscribers. The Associates, founded in 1929 to support the collections of the Library, continue in vigorous good health, and I hope the hundreds of current members will derive much pleasure and interest from this new publication. The idea is to present aspects from different perspectives of this great library system to our many friends and to all those with an interest. To be published annually, each issue will focus on a theme closely connected to the work of the Yale University Library. This first issue of Yale Library Studies, which takes library architecture at Yale as its theme, illustrates the integral importance of the Library to the University both as part of its physical fabric and built environment, and at the core of the educational experience. The second issue, planned for 2010, will consider some of the distinctive collections of the Library and the collectors who put them together.

The many buildings that have housed libraries at Yale over the past three hundred years have differed, sometimes radically, in form, size, and architectural style. They have ranged from the private home of the Reverend Samuel Russel in eighteenth-century Branford to those two great monuments of twentieth-century Yale, the Sterling Memorial and Beinecke Libraries, which are separated by only a few yards of space and just over thirty years, but also by a stylistic and cultural gulf. The most successful library buildings have been those which, in the words of the Dean of the School of Architecture, Robert A.M. Stern, "cast special light on Yale's sense of itself as a community of scholars." To use the words of another contributor to this volume, Aric Lasher, Architect Principal at Hammond Beeby Rupert Ainge, the firm that transformed the former Cross Campus Library into the new Bass Library, the best library buildings take their place "within an architectural program thoroughly enmeshed with Yale's status and identity."

Just in case there could be any mistake about Yale's status and identity, it sometimes seems that the University's architects and planners, at least before about 1940, were unable to see a stone wall without carving upon it some improving message. The most quoted inscription from the many emblazoned on the walls of Sterling Memorial Library reads: "The Library is the Heart of the University." It is striking how this sentiment is borne out in the central location of this largest and most monumental of all the library buildings, with its towering presence taking up nearly a whole block between High and York Streets. A question that has exercised more than one University Librarian, however, is how far that truth so evident in stone and metal and wood manifests itself in the interior life of Yale. To what extent do the Library's many buildings embody the ideals and aspirations of the University? Do the scholars and students who use these buildings find in them not just the books and collections but also the environment they need to help them teach and study and learn? And what, in a twenty-first-century library system, is the relationship between the virtual environment found on the computer or handheld device and the physical built environment? It is not accidental that the technologists who build systems for the transmittal, linking, and preservation of information refer to their own "architecture."

Yale's educational and intellectual values find plentiful representation in the architectural embellishments of its library buildings. The superabundant detail of Sterling Memorial Library alone ranges from the playful and the downright frivolous to the informative and aspirational. A favorite with tourists is the gargoyle-like stone corbel in the exhibit corridor showing a student hunched over a book that reads "U R A JOKE." Some other beloved *jeux d'esprit* include the mop and pail carved over the lintel of a janitorial closet and two figures speaking on a telephone, circa 1929, above the superannuated phone booth near the Linonia and Brothers Reading Room. Scenes from the history of Yale, New Haven, and Connecticut and images from the Library's collections abound in the pictorial windows and wood and stone carvings, beginning with the ministers laying books on a table "to found a college in this Colony" in 1701 and proceeding through the unseemly fight over the books that ensued when the college moved from Saybrook to New Haven in 1718. Both episodes are memorialized in stone carvings by René P. Chambellan on the side of the nave below the magnificent windows by G. Owen Bonawit. For the aspirational, few sights can beat the inscriptions on the panels above the entrance on High Street showing quotations from ancient languages of the world, each in its own script. International and language studies have flourished and increased at Yale over the succeeding decades, and the global message they convey is even more appropriate today than it was when the building opened in 1930. Equally, it is a tribute to the adaptability of James Gamble Rogers's design that a spacious room on the first floor with elaborate wooden carving and a decorated plaster ceiling, once the home of Yale memorabilia and then of the Arts of the Book Collection, now houses a new global reading room. The room delivers in a new way on the promise of the High Street frieze, creating a portal for visitors to find out about Yale's multifarious international activities, and for librarians to help faculty members and students prepare for teaching and study abroad.

"Everything was new and wonderful," writes the late Marjorie Wynne of her first impressions of Sterling Memorial Library in her essay "Crossing Wall." She then goes on to describe the process of transferring her collections, and some of her allegiance, to the contrasting modernist splendor of architect Gordon Bunshaft's Beinecke Rare Book and Manuscript Library. Sterling Memorial Library honored its benefactor with a cathedral of learning, where the books and treasures contained in the stacks and vaults and on reading room shelves were represented first by thousands of catalog cards in their exquisitely carved wooden cabinets under the arched enclaves resembling side chapels off the nave, and by the awe-inspiring circulation desk presided over by Eugene Savage's emblematic *Alma Mater*. Just a few very elegant exhibit cases were placed in the nave to display books. The Beinecke Library, by contrast, reflected the learned collecting interests of the three bibliophile Beinecke brothers by displaying its rare books in a great glass tower at the center of the building, ensuring that books are the unmissable first sight to greet the visitor. Both buildings have become iconic monuments on Yale's central campus, and both have outlasted some of the assumptions about libraries that their architects incorporated into the designs. Each in its own way, however, has withstood major tests of time and has proved responsive to evolving ways of using library buildings and collections.

Essays in this inaugural volume of Yale Library Studies explore several of the creative architectural solutions to the Library's changing functions, notably in the Bass Library and Centerbrook Architects' renovation and new building at the Lewis Walpole Library, described by Mark Simon. But the combination of library innovation with new uses of space is found throughout the system. In the Cushing/Whitney Medical Library, acquiring large quantities of serials and other publications in electronic form instead of print has freed space to create new areas for quiet study and small group collaboration. There is new space to house the extraordinary study collection of brains bequeathed by the eminent surgeon Harvey Cushing, and there are several special collections such as the Consumer Health collection for patients and their families, end-of-life resources, teaching resources in the education collection, and a new reading corner for popular resources of interest to the medical community. These most recent developments continue the evolution of the Cushing/Whitney Medical Library, which includes the timeless ambience of the Historical Medical Library's reading room designed by Grosvenor Atterbury in 1941 as part of the first dedicated medical library in the Yale system.

Separate libraries within Yale's system often embody different approaches to the functions of studying, teaching, and learning, according to the different perspectives of different disciplines. The hidden and inaccessible nature of the former Art + Architecture Library seemed like a travesty of the light and display that ought to characterize a library of the visual arts. Now, opened up to the forefront of the Rudolph building by the late Charles Gwathmey and not only serving art, history of art, and architecture but also incorporating the Drama Library and the Arts of the Book Collection, the new Robert B. Haas Family Arts Library acts, in Gwathmey's words, "as the common intellectual domain where students from the various disciplines would share and engage." This beautiful, airy space also benefits from developments in technology that enabled the library to digitize the Visual Resources Collection (VRC) of more than a quarter of a million slides: a program that facilitates teaching from the collection and also liberates space that would have been taken up by the wooden slide cabinets, to make way for a special collections reading room and exhibit area. The slides are housed at the Library Shelving Facility, from where they can be delivered when needed, and VRC professionals meanwhile work with users at what may be seen as one of several nodes of digital service in the Library system, both within the Arts Library and with faculty in their offices and classrooms.

Renovation of the East Asia Library on the second floor of Sterling provided newly equipped seminar rooms that are well used by classes working with collections in both physical and digital form. Here again, Rogers's flexible architecture enabled Hammond Beeby Rupert Ainge (working simultaneously on the Bass Library) to create an environment appropriately influenced by Japanese and Chinese design, combining shelving, study, and classroom spaces. The most spectacular adaptation within Sterling, though, is surely the Irving S. Gilmore Music Library designed by Shepley Bulfinch Richardson and Abbott. Opened in 1998, it has three stories for teaching, study, exhibits, and offices centered on a soaring curved stairway and set within the taller of two inner courtyards in the original building. If successful architecture marries form to function, one especially pleasing example was the occasion in 2005 when the Yale Collegium Musicum gathered in the Music Library to sing for the trustees of the Yale Library Associates from the newly acquired table edition of Purcell's *Lachrimae*.

In the northern part of the Yale campus, the adaptive reuse of the Sterling Divinity Quadrangle in 2000–2001 by the architecture firm of Kliment and Halsband resulted in a renovated Divinity School Library with more space for people. The new library retains its elegant reading rooms and now includes teaching spaces, group study rooms, and the Ministry Resource Center, a collection supporting the practice of ministry. To my knowledge it is the only library with its own chapel (the octagonal Henri Nouwen Chapel) and organ. The Graves Forestry and Environmental Studies Library is now situated in a magnificent new building, Kroon Hall (2009), the first building on the Yale campus to qualify for a Leadership in Energy and Environmental Design (LEED) platinum rating, the highest rating for a sustainable building. At the School of Management, plans now being prepared for a building designed by Norman Foster include a prominently located three-level library with a technology and media center, workstations for high-end financial and management databases, group and individual study spaces, and a multipurpose service desk.

Looking further ahead, when Yale builds the two new residential colleges on Prospect Street designed by Robert A.M. Stern, the Seeley G. Mudd Library (a building designed by the firm of Roth and Moore and opened in 1983) and Urban Hall (1957), housing, respectively, the Government Documents and Information Center and the Social Science Library and Statistical Laboratory. In their stead, positioned on Prospect Street opposite the new colleges, will be a combined science and social science library with the Statistical Laboratory and classrooms in the same building. This new and bold conception of a library will bring together disciplines and study habits that are usually separated both physically and conceptually. The necessary preface to moving the Kline Science Library out of Phillip Johnson's 1965 Kline Biology Tower will be a period of a few years during which both coexist in reconfigured space in the current science library. Essential to this experimental phase will be the move of a very large proportion of their printed volumes to Bruce Scott's Library Shelving Facility, whose incorporation into the life of the University Library (much contested when it opened in 1998) has become a precondition for the Library's successful expansion of its collections and development of services.

The interplay of electronic, virtual collections and the physical environment in the modern experience of the library has opened up a whole series of opportunities within the generous and varied framework of the Yale University Library system. It is instructive to see how space freed by the removal or compression of fixed furnishings and printed reference works has engendered uses that put people in touch with the Library's collections in new ways. Our architects have designed for us places where library staff can connect more directly than ever with their users, and new entry points to the library experience for faculty and students. In Sterling, with card catalog cabinets emptied and removal of the freestanding cabinets into which the cards had overflowed (inexorably, as it must have seemed until the beginning of an electronic catalog in the 1980s), there are enticing possibilities. The exhibit cases now stand in the enclaves, where they are used by faculty and students as well as librarians to mount thought-provoking displays. The carved, built-in cabinets may lend themselves one day to repurposing as exhibit cases. Meanwhile, there is a hum of activity, including classes gathered round the exhibits, and, for a week in the summer of 2009, filmmaking. On the other side of the nave are computer terminals that would have been equally unimaginable when the building opened in 1930. The Beinecke Library, a treasure box designed above all for the preservation, display, and quiet study of its great collections, now welcomes poetry readings, musical performances, and school groups, with undergraduate classes poring over manuscripts in its classrooms and working with curators on electronic versions.

Modern library buildings house working collections and rare, distinctive materials carefully safeguarded for posterity, along with staff who provide and mediate access to material in all formats. Laura Tatum's essay about Yale's architectural archives that preserve the work of some of Yale's and New Haven's most important architects and designers, in both paper and electronic form, is an appropriate reminder. The essence of a great research library consists of both the collections that students and scholars come to study and the expert staff who preserve and build those collections and make them available for generations to come. Danuta A. Nitecki describes how the concept of the "Learning Commons" has been developed in the beautiful new Anne T. and Robert M. Bass Library and adjacent Wright Reading Room, named to honor William H. Wright II. This underground haven of quiet study mixed with teaching, social learning, and creative use of technology, in surroundings created with self-effacing architectural genius by the firm of Hammond Beeby Rupert Ainge, embodies many if not all of the aspirations of a modern university library. Nitecki's essay in some ways brackets this volume with the essay by Margaret K. Powell, who reveals the eighteenth-century visions of study and sociable scholarly discourse among transcendently beautiful surroundings that Horace Walpole and his circle elevated, at Strawberry Hill, to a way of life and a kind of art form. Walpole's notions of the exquisite and his lifelong devotion to collecting and scholarly study, memorialized as they are in one of the many libraries that Yale has restored and expanded in recent years, receive a fitting match in the extraordinary library environments enjoyed by twenty-first-century students, scholars, and staff at Yale.

I wish to extend most cordial thanks to all the contributors to this volume, and to those who have worked hard on editing and designing it: Geoffrey Little, the editor; Christa Sammons, who helped edit a number of the essays based on many years' experience with the *Yale University Library Gazette*; Christina Coffin, Vadim Staklo, and their colleagues at Yale University Press; Tina Weiner, Susan Matheson, Tiffany Sprague, Lesley Baier, and John Gambell, who provided helpful advice when we first contemplated this venture; and many others, both members of the Yale Library Associates and members of the Library staff, who have contributed advice and good ideas. This acknowledgment would not be complete without a sad note of farewell to two contributors: Marjorie Wynne died in April 2009, and Charles Gwathmey died in August 2009. Miss Wynne's great legacy to the Library was a lifetime of distinguished work as a leading research librarian, continuing as a friend and mentor to numerous members of the staff until her death. And Mr. Gwathmey, an illustrious alumnus of the Yale School of Architecture, has left us a beautiful new Arts Library that has already proved hugely successful and will surely stand the test of time.

Dixwell Renewal Project Site Plan, 1968.
Richard D. Johnson Slide Collection. Manuscripts and Archives, Yale University Library.

ROBERT A.M. STERN

Library Architecture at Yale

For the simple reason that its very existence is owed to the gift in 1701 of books by Connecticut clergy, and in 1718 of a significant gift of nine crates of books and other assets by Elihu Yale (1649–1721), a Boston-born businessman residing in England whose fortune was made in the East India trade, there is nothing more important to Yale than its library, or more properly libraries, which now are almost as diverse in number as the subjects taught in the University.[1] As libraries at Yale have evolved over more than three hundred years' time, they constitute a treasury of buildings and rooms that cast special light on Yale's sense of itself as a community of scholars.[2]

The original college met at Branford, Connecticut, but Elihu Yale's gift inspired the decision to relocate to New Haven. Generous though the gift was, the fortunes of the newly formed college were nonetheless modest, as reflected in the simple three-and-a-half-story building (1718, demolished 1782) [fig. 1] containing a combined dining room and chapel, suites of student rooms, and a library it constructed on an eight-acre site that the town of New Haven made available facing the green at the corner of Chapel and College Streets.[3]

As the college prospered, it expanded, and in 1763 its library and chapel were given a combined home in a new building, set partially behind College House and next to Connecticut Hall (1750), the first of the buildings to constitute a "brick row" that would grow over the next half-century according to the plan of the painter and amateur architect Colonel John Trumbull (1756–1843), who proposed to house the continually expanding library together with classrooms in a building realized in 1803 as the Lyceum [fig. 2].[4]

In 1825 the library moved yet again, this time to the attic of a new chapel, but it was to be another twenty years before the College would undertake its first purpose-built library (1842–46) [figs. 3–4], calling on the services of local architect Henry Austin (1804–1891), who may or may not have collaborated on its design with the more established Ithiel Town (1784–1844) or his better-known partner, Alexander Jackson Davis (1803–1892). James O'Gorman, in his monograph on Austin, points to an earlier Davis design for a "Grecian Pantheon, obviously inspired in form if not precise classical precedent by Thomas Jefferson's work at the University of Virginia," a design possibly prepared in 1835 at the behest of Aaron N. Skinner (B.A. 1823), a prominent New Haven citizen who asked for a "chaste and classical plan for a College Library,"[5] a design that would be criticized on functional grounds by P. L. Forbes of the New York Society Library, who objected to the rotunda and advocated a rectangle lined with book alcoves. Forbes's criticism led to a new design, possibly the work of Town or more likely that of Davis, who in a March 1842 journal entry recorded his work on a "Library for Yale College, Gothic Style." As O'Gorman suggests: "If Town

Frontispiece. Beineke Plaza, 1963
Ezra Stoller
© *Esto*.

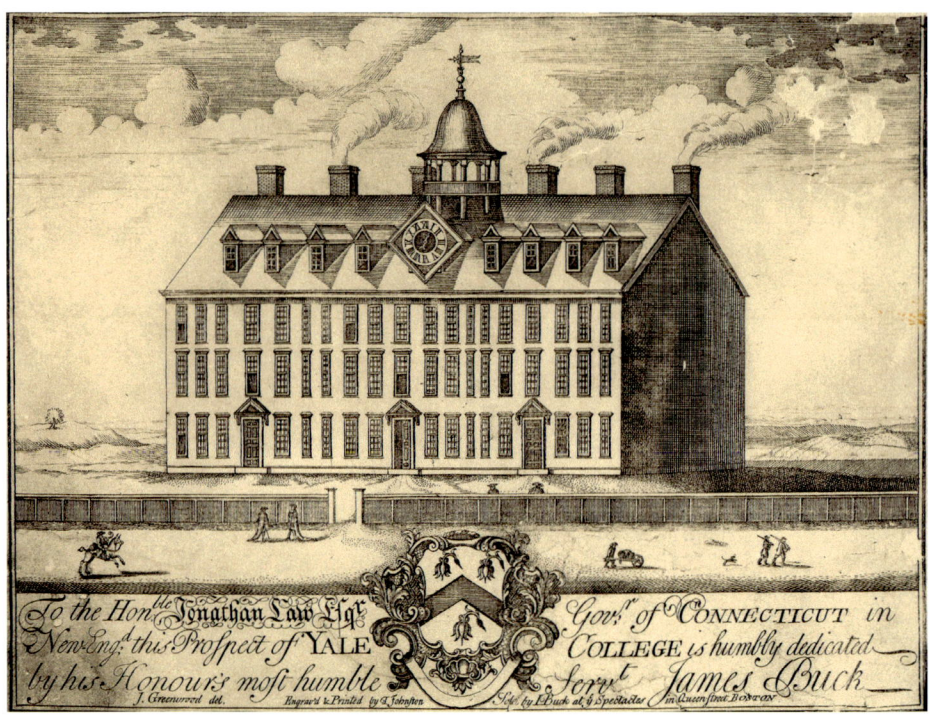

Figure 1. Yale College (1718–82), c. 1745 by T. Johnson.
Yale University Buildings and Grounds Photographs (RU 703).
Manuscripts and Archives, Yale University Library.

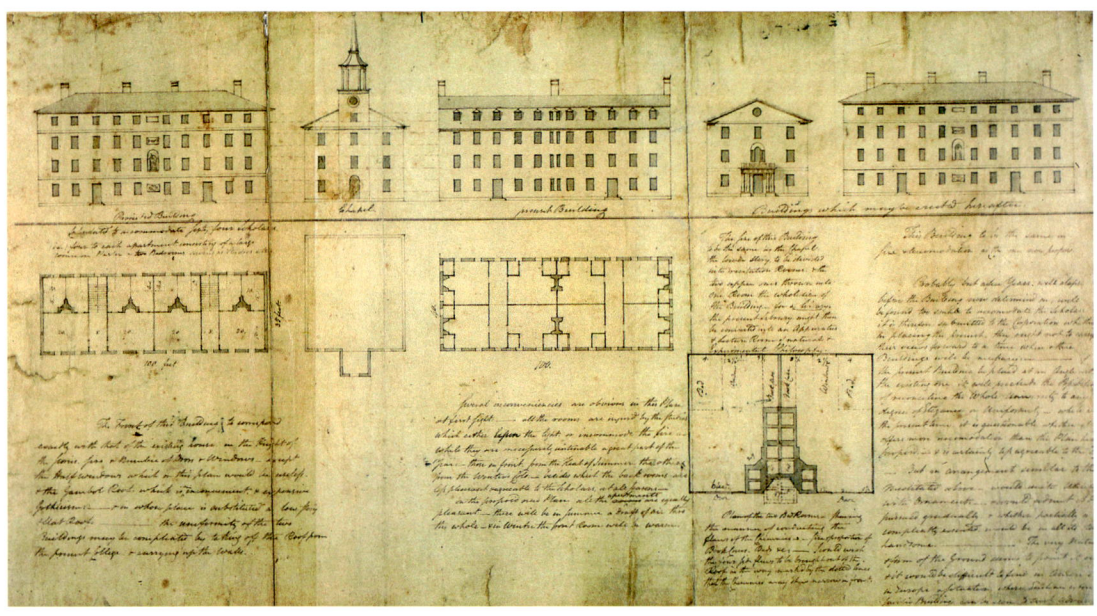

Figure 2. John Trumbull's 1794 plan for Old Brick Row.
Architectural Drawings and Maps of Yale University Buildings and Grounds (RU 1).
Manuscripts and Archives.

Figure 3. Engraving of Henry Austin's College Library, 1854,
from an album owned by Jacob Brown Harris, B.A. 1854.
Manuscripts and Archives.

Figure 4. College Library interior, 1880.
Pictures of Dwight Hall, Yale University, c. 1846–1937. Manuscripts and Archives.

had set a plan, Davis must have been working on the sections and elevations, but with that entry both Town and Davis vanish from the written documentation regarding the design of the building," seemingly making way for Austin, who was ultimately put in charge of the project.[6] Austin may well have competed along with others such as Town for the commission, but O'Gorman intimates that some backstage financial dealings may have led to the job going to the comparatively untested and unknown Austin, whose previous executed work included little more than a row of villas in Trenton, New Jersey.[7]

Inspired, in all likelihood, by King's College Chapel, Cambridge, the design of the new brownstone College Library, which also bears some similarities to Harvard's first library building, Gore Hall (1838), consisted of a central, chapel-like mass oriented east-west, connected by hyphens to two smaller dependencies, an arrangement that was less calibrated to the prevailing standards of library science than to the need to provide uniquely defined rooms for the College's various literary societies: the Linonia and the Brothers in Unity in the wings, and the Calliopean located in the south hyphen. These societies had grown up over time, collecting light fiction to attract members. The dominant central, chapel-like mass provided a nave-like reading room lit by clerestory windows and lower book-lined side aisles.

Austin's College Library was set back on the original eight-acre campus block, no doubt because Brick Row was pretty much filled up. But there were other reasons for this decision, including fear of fire, which had become an issue after two severe fires in New Haven and one in Harvard's library. By siting the library away from other buildings, the chance of mass conflagration was greatly reduced. Moreover, the site chosen lay across the street from a firehouse. In the long run, the choice of site for the new library proved crucial, marking a turning point in Yale's growth from a provincial college to a major university. The placement of the library on the opposite end of the college land from Brick Row proclaimed an ambition to create a campus with a library and not a chapel as its center. Ezekiel Porter Belden (B.A. 1844), in *Sketches of Yale College* (1843), was perhaps the first to articulate this idea when he wrote that the library's site at the back of the block and at the end of a new mid-block street to the west (Library Street) positioned the library as "the central thing in the whole establishment."[8]

College Library was an important breakthrough for Yale in at least two other ways. On the most basic level of institutional structure, it was Yale's first building designed solely for the purpose of holding books and readers, elevating the University Library to the status of a department equal to other academic departments. Moreover, in adapting a style that was laden with associations of medieval scholasticism, College Library lifted the standard of building accommodation from the functionally straightforward into the realm of self-conscious and deliberate expressionism given that by the time of its commission, red brick Georgian had come to be uncomfortably associated with the utilitarianism of typical mill structures proliferating all over New England, a point Patrick Pinnell

Figure 5. Chittenden Hall before the construction of Linsly Hall. *Yale University Buildings and Grounds Photographs (RU 703). Manuscripts and Archives.*

(B.A. 1971, M.ARCH. 1974) puts bluntly in his architectural guide to the campus published in 1999: "As more factories sprung up . . . Yale . . . became less enchanted with [its] aging brick boxes, which bore more than a passing resemblance to the new intruders. Yale scientist Benjamin Silliman [B.A. 1796, M.A. 1799] tried to justify the Row structures as 'manufactories, not indeed of cotton and wool, but of mind,' but that spin attempt went nowhere fast. By the 1830s, the College clearly had what in the 1990s is known as an image problem."[9]

The Gothic style was seen not only as an antidote to utilitarianism but also as a means, as contemporary Lyman Hotchkiss Bagg (B.A. 1869) observed, to construct a building with "pretensions to architectural beauty."[10] That is to say, it reflected a growing realization that architectural style was an issue not of tectonic inevitability but of rhetorical intention. And Elizabeth Mills Brown, in her pioneering guide to New Haven's architecture and urbanism, states that "although later generations, raised on Ruskinian ideas about true Medieval construction, scorned these plaster vaults and wooden pinnacles," the building "was an exciting herald of a new Yale . . . tempered by romantic brown shadows and Tudor towers, slim and agile as minarets."[11]

Not every student was enthusiastic about Yale's Gothic turn, which was soon to include Peter B. Wight's (1838–1925) Ruskin-inspired Street Hall (1864–66). As Catherine Lynn (PH.D. 1980) points out, one outspoken undergraduate, George C. Holt (B.A. 1866), objected in the *Yale Literary Magazine* to its introduction on the grounds of stylistic unity: "Yale is no Gothic College, and it wants no Gothic buildings."[12] Ironically, more than thirty-five years later, Holt would be a member of the building committee that, as Lynn puts it, "directed Yale architecture on its most radical stylistic aberration before the High Modern era, its plunge into the grandeur of Beaux-Arts Classicism for the Bicentennial Buildings."[13]

Though significantly larger than any other Yale building at the time, College Library nonetheless soon filled up with books and readers, leading to the need for expansion in the form of an annex, at last realized in 1889 as Chittenden Hall [fig. 5], the design of which, like practically all Yale's buildings of the second half of the nineteenth century, was medieval in inspiration but not specifically Gothic. It was, in fact, designed in the fashionable style of the day—the Richardsonian Romanesque—by New York architect J. Cleveland Cady (1837–1919), who was responsible for eleven of Yale's late nineteenth-century buildings, including North Sheffield Hall (1872–73, demolished 1967) and the first home of the Peabody Museum of Natural History (1873–76, demolished 1917), as well as the Law School building (1897, now known as Hendrie Hall), Dwight Hall (1885–86, demolished 1926), Berkeley Hall (1893–94, demolished 1933), and the Whitman Memorial Gateway (1894).[14]

Chittenden was intended to be far bigger than what was actually executed. A committee assembled to plan library expansion in 1883 proposed wrapping Austin's College Library, which was coming to be known as the Old Library, with new construction on three sides to be realized in three stages. According to the plan, the use of Austin's College Library was to continue, but it was not clear for how much longer, given that Chittenden was promoted not as an addition, but as "part of the future."[15] Cady's plan, in fact, shows no sign of Austin's library, which it seems to swallow up.

Austin's College Library was built at a time when upperclassmen were permitted to borrow books and take them to their rooms, a virtual necessity given that the building was practically unheated and had no artificial lighting, limiting its use to daylight hours.[16] But the growth of the library's collections and the increasing seriousness of the College's academic life meant that Chittenden would be built for a collection that did not circulate, so its principal feature was a generously sized octagonal reading room, forty-five feet across, seating ninety scholars who enjoyed the comforts of central heating and in daytime were bathed in the glow of a memorial window designed by Tiffany and in evening had the advantages of gas light, converted to electricity in 1896.

Soon enough Chittenden, too, became overcrowded. But Cady's original plan for a balancing wing on the north side of the Old Library was not followed, and instead Charles Coolidge Haight (1841–1917), known for his notable Gothic work for Columbia College on its midtown campus and for the General Theological Seminary, both in New York, was awarded the commission for what would become Linsly Hall, a building that returned to the Gothic style of the Old Library.[17] Linsly was conceived principally as an efficient book repository for what had become a significant research library.

Haight was awarded the commission of Linsly Hall in a design competition held in 1905, when the University invited a formidable group of architects to submit proposals: the partnership of John Mead Howells (1868–1959) and I. N. Phelps Stokes (1867–1944), Robert H. Robertson (1849–1919) and Robert Burnside Potter (1869–1934), and the newly established but well-connected partnership of William Adams Delano (1874–1960, B.A. 1895, B.F.A. 1907, M.A. HON. 1939) and Chester H. Aldrich (1871–1940). Significantly, all three firms submitted robustly Gothic designs, reflecting the newly minted English Collegiate Gothic style that the firm of Cope and Stewardson had introduced at the University of Pennsylvania (1893), Princeton (1896), and the Washington University of St. Louis (1899). Of the competition entries, only that of Delano and Aldrich proposed to save the central portion of the Old Library, suggesting its reuse as the main entrance hall and book delivery room. James Gamble Rogers (1867–1947, B.A. 1889, M.A. HON. 1921) was also invited to submit a design, but he dropped out of the competition because he was "unable to find a solution of the difficulties of the requirements."[18]

Although Haight's premiated proposal was intended to stretch to the north, as had Cady's earlier Chittenden library proposal, the portion of the design realized as Linsly Hall (1907) lay between the Old Library and Chittenden Hall, and it was little more than a connector between them, providing six decks of self-supporting metal book stacks as well as conference and study rooms. From the point of view of stylistic expression, however, its importance cannot be overemphasized: it distanced itself from the no longer fashionable Romanesque of Chittenden Hall and returned to the English Gothic of the Old Library.

While the decision to build Linsly Hall and the acceptance of Haight's plan for a vast expansion in the future presumed to accept the continuing value of what was coming to be known as the Old Campus as the appropriate home for the library, consideration was also given by Yale's governing body, the Corporation, to a site on the so-called New Campus, or University Square, where the monumentally Classical Bicentennial Buildings (John Merven Carrère [1858–1911] and Thomas Hastings [1860–1929], 1901) had been recently realized, and the location that John Russell Pope (1874–1937, M.A. HON. 1924) would advocate for a new library in his 1919 proposed campus plan.

The relocation to the New Campus site, lying between Elm and Grove Streets, was put to the side because Yale did not yet own all the property on the block. Nonetheless, its likely availability in the future called into question the decision to expand the library on the Old Campus, where there was little room for growth. Some, recognizing the increasing importance of the Sheffield Scientific School to the expanding University as a whole, urged that the library be built even farther to the north on the Hillhouse Estate, diagonally across Grove Street from the Bicentennial Buildings, which were now seen as the new center of an enlarged, multiblock campus. At the same time, there was a growing expression of sentiment on behalf of the Old Library, which would be lost in the fulfillment of the Cady plan, leading 231 members of the class of 1905 to petition for its preservation. The case of the library's future location and the preservation

Figure 6.
John Russell Pope's
1919 proposal for
the New Campus.
From Yale University:
A Plan for Its Future
Building.
*Manuscripts and
Archives.*

of the Old Library was taken up by the *Yale Alumni Weekly*: "The old library with its alcoves, its sympathetic architecture, the indefinite charm of its associations and history, will furnish for a very long time just those quiet places for study and research, for composition and creation, for a very considerable body of men, which ought to be available in any home of scholarship."[19]

The addition of Linsly Hall proved merely a stopgap measure, and there was no getting around the fact that the library needed to grow dramatically again. New standards of size, if not efficiency, had been established by the completion of McKim, Mead and White's Low Memorial Library (1895–97) as the centerpiece of Columbia's new campus in uptown Manhattan and, even more tellingly, with the construction in 1915 of Horace Trumbauer and Associates' Widener Memorial Library at Harvard. In each case these libraries not only significantly exceeded Yale's capacity for storing books and accommodating readers but also, by their sheer physical presence, conveyed an impression of scholarly commitment that Yale's agglomeration of library buildings did not.[20] In 1917 John Russell Pope was invited by Francis Patrick Garvan (B.A. 1897, M.A. HON. 1922) and Harry Payne Whitney (B.A. 1894), who were instrumental in Yale's acquiring land for expansion, to prepare a plan for the University's future growth.[21]

Pope's proposal included a new library on the so-called New Campus, a building that, had it been realized, would loom over the Bicentennial Buildings as

Figure 7. John Russell Pope's 1919 design for the University Library on the New Campus. *From* Yale University: A Plan for Its Future Building. *Manuscripts and Archives.*

a massive Gothic-style cathedral of learning [fig. 6]. The plan also called for the creation of a grand east-west mall along the axis of Wall Street, a minor avenue. Pope's English Collegiate Gothic library, influenced by King's College Chapel and Great St. Mary's Church, Cambridge, and by Magdalen College, Oxford, decisively echoed Austin's College Library, but at a vast scale [fig. 7]. However, the bold nature of this proposal and that for the expansion of the campus as a whole, which had not experienced a master plan for one hundred years, since the time of Colonel Trumbull, appears to have met some resistance by the Corporation, which convened a committee of three architects—Cass Gilbert (1859–1934), most recently famous for his skyscraping Gothic-style Woolworth Building in New York (1913), Bertram Grosvenor Goodhue (1869–1924), one of the country's preeminent architects specializing in the Gothic style, but increasingly daring in his interpretation of that style, and James Gamble Rogers—to advise them on Pope's plan. Ultimately, Paul Philippe Cret (1876–1945), a French-born Classicist, replaced Gilbert, and William Adams Delano replaced Rogers, the latter no doubt stepping aside because of his having just been commissioned by Mrs. Anna M. Harkness (1837–1926) to design the Gothic-style memorial tower and residential complex (1917–21) that would become the cornerstone of Yale's residential college system.

Not surprisingly, Pope, hurt by the Corporation's decision to appoint architects to second-guess him, resisted their suggestions, most notably one proposing that the library be built on the York Street site where he had called for a new gym. Pope stepped aside, and responsibility for planning the new campus was turned over to Rogers, who agreed to not take on new commissions for Yale buildings beyond the Harkness Memorial. Rogers developed a new plan for the University expansion that was approved in 1924.[22]

While it is not within the scope of this essay to assess Pope's master plan, it is clear that his design for the new library, though bold, seemed rather longer on ceremony than utility, suffering from the same limitations as Austin's earlier nave-based design, a building that Pope admired and whose preservation he successfully lobbied for. However, Pope's library design possessed, as Pinnell writes, "enormous, taciturn reserve"[23] that would later be revealed in his Payne Whitney Gymnasium (1932), which the architect would be commissioned to design as a kind of consolation prize, and for which he would employ a similar arrangement, packing weight rooms, squash courts, and the like into what had been originally conceived as a tower of book stacks, thus earning the building the affectionate nickname "Cathedral of Sweat." Pope would show Yale a much more gentle side of his talent in the design of Calhoun College (1932).[24]

Although Rogers was put in charge of Yale's evolving building program as supervisory architect, responsibility for the most important new building to be undertaken in the 1920s, the Sterling Memorial Library, went to Bertram Grosvenor Goodhue.[25] Goodhue, who from 1892 until 1913 had been in partnership with Ralph Adams Cram (1863–1942), was far better known than Rogers, and his widely recognized name was attractive to the trustees of the estate of John William Sterling (1844–1918, B.A. 1864), a lawyer with close connections to Standard Oil whose bequest would pay for the construction of a new library along with many other benefactions to the University. While Goodhue's reputation lay principally as architect of Gothic-style churches, by the late 1910s he was engaged in the design of a wide variety of building types that led him to search for modern versions of various historical styles. He experimented with the Spanish Colonial at the Panama-California Exposition in San Diego (1915), with Classicism in his National Academy of Sciences in Washington, D.C. (1919–24), and with the Mughal in the Los Angeles Public Library (1921–26), and in his Nebraska State Capitol (1920–32) he achieved a free eclecticism of form that was quickly embraced by American architects as an important milestone on the path toward stylistic modernity. According to Patrick Pinnell, Goodhue even prepared a Classical scheme for the Sterling Library, but it was soon clear to him and to his clients that the new building was to be an essay in Gothic, albeit a modern version that Goodhue hoped to evolve.[26] Writing in 1924 to the English architect and fellow progressive Gothicist Giles Gilbert Scott (1880–1960), Goodhue stated that although the Yale library "has to be in the 'Gothic manner' . . . [as] most of the other buildings at Yale are—or their authors and owners think they are," he, who had lost his "taste for 'straight' Gothic," was "hoping to 'put over' something that won't be, although it will look like, Gothic."[27]

Pope had situated his library cheek by jowl with the Bicentennial Buildings. Goodhue's library, as he along with Cret and Rogers had recommended to the Corporation, was to be sited where Pope had proposed a new gymnasium, at the west end of a new mall, or cross campus, that would not lie along the axis of Wall Street as Pope had proposed but would instead bisect the block between Wall Street on the north and Elm Street on the south, permitting the new library to be part of a series of linked quadrangles realized over time as property was acquired and funds became available so that the library complex as a whole would eventually fill the block between Wall, Elm, High, and York Streets. This would come to pass when the construction of Pope's Payne Whitney Gymnasium on Tower Parkway permitted the demolition of the old gym and swimming pool south of Sterling Library to give way to Trumbull College (1929–33).

Despite the bravura of his letter to Scott, Goodhue's scheme evolved slowly from a more literal, picturesque Gothic to a dense, abstract Gothic composition that would have had at its center a formidable cubic mass incorporating at ground floor a main hall leading to various special reading rooms, the delivery desk, and an exhibit hall with, to one side, a quadrangle ringed by seminar rooms [figs. 8–9]. To the north, across Wall Street, where Pope had situated his proposed library, Goodhue proposed to locate the Graduate School that, like Pope's library but at a much gentler scale, would screen the intrusive Classicism of the Bicentennial Buildings from Yale's renewed Gothicism [fig. 10].

Aaron Betsky (B.A. 1979, M.ARCH. 1983), in his monograph on Rogers, describes Goodhue's library as a "sixteen-story fortress of bookstacks" rising "from a low base of reading rooms," "a solid block with narrow slits through which one can imagine scholars shooting arrows of knowledge at the infidel undergraduates."[28] Nonetheless, as Betsky points out, "the stripped-down gothicism of the proposed building, its scale buttressed by picturesque contextual elements and its ceremonial spaces suppressed in favor of private places of reflection and functional circulatory nodes, was closer to the work of James Gamble Rogers than to some of Goodhue's other work during the period."[29] The road to design resolution proved difficult for Goodhue, whose proposals failed to impress either Rogers or John Farwell (B.A. 1879), the chairman of the Corporation Committee on the Architectural Plan. But, as Betsky writes: "Eventually, Rogers worked through a mutual friend, with the result that Goodhue did change the design presented to the Corporation Committee on the Architectural Plan. Whatever developments might have occurred after this conversation between two of the most successful builders of institutions and manipulators of gothic styles in a modern mode were cut off by Goodhue's untimely death in April 1924."[30]

With Goodhue dead, the job did not continue in the hands of members of the late architect's office, reconstituted as Goodhue Associates, but was instead handed over to Rogers, whom Goodhue had all along suspected had wanted the commission. As Goodhue's associates related it, their leader had warned them that Rogers was opposed "to the employment of other than Yale graduates as

Figure 8. *Design for a University Library* by Bertram Grosvenor Goodhue, 1924.
From Bertram Grosvenor Goodhue: Architect and Master of Many Arts
(New York: American Institute of Architects, 1925). Used with permission.

Figure 9. Goodhue's University Library from the Cross Campus.
From Bertram Grosvenor Goodhue: Architect and Master of Many Arts
(New York: American Institute of Architects, 1925). Used with permission.

Figure 10. "Bird's Eye View of New Cross Campus" showing the proposed design for the new library. *From* Yale Alumni Weekly *(February 1, 1924)*.

architects for work at Yale University."[31] In 1928 the University was able to buy the holdout property on the block so that Goodhue's conception of what Richard Oliver, in his monograph on the architect, has described as "a medieval village gathered about a castle of books," could be realized.[32]

Goodhue's impressive early work notwithstanding, it fell to Rogers to give definitive shape to the enormous new library building originally intended for five million books as well as study rooms and offices.[33] Rogers maintained Goodhue's most daring innovation, which was not one of style but of organization: this was to be a "skyscraping" library, with books stacked in a tower [fig. 11]. But he increased the length of his tower and pushed it farther west, situating it above the book delivery room so that readers' calls for materials could be quickly sent in a pneumatic tube for retrieval by staff in the stacks and brought down by dumbwaiter to the main desk. Passenger elevators were also provided to facilitate the movement between the various floors of the book tower for those faculty permitted access as well as staff and book carts. To a considerable extent this was the system put in place by Carrère and Hastings in their New York Public Library (1897–1911), but in that building the reading room was placed at the top of the building so that the book stacks were not liberated from the mass as an expressed tower, an idea first employed in Goodhue's Los Angeles Public Library.[34] The frankly expressed independent stack tower fulfilled the wishes of Andrew Keogh (1869–1953), the University Librarian, who from the first

Figure 11. Sterling Memorial Library from the Cross Campus in the 1940s. *Sterling Memorial Library, Yale University, Photographs (RU 696). Manuscripts and Archives.*

wanted a factory of learning and not a monument to learning, as Columbia's Low Library notoriously was, and who requested that all reading rooms be on the main floor for ease of access by undergraduates and scholars. This decision proved inspired, impressing Rogers fully two years before the commission was his.[35] However, as Betsky writes, "In the end, the Sterling trustees and the Yale administration, despite all of their lip service to Keogh's 'factory of learning,' preferred to take out six tiers of book stacks, reducing the height of the tower by fifty feet, rather than compromise on the level of detail and the overall quality of the new library." After all, one of the trustees had already pointed out, the building was meant to be a memorial to Sterling, and, as Farwell noted, the focus of the vastly expanded campus. The functions of the library would be housed efficiently, but they were not the reason for the building. When the drop in the height of the tower exposed the mechanical equipment on the roof to view from the campus, money was quickly found to house these unsightly technological components by covering them with a lead-coated copper Gothic village. In the end, the building was so grand that Keogh wanted to carve an inscription on the front that would read: "This is NOT the Yale Library. That is inside."[36] Sterling Memorial Library was dedicated in April 1931, eleven years after it was initiated.

Rogers clarified Goodhue's plan. Pushing the tower to the west enabled the octagonal hall to be reshaped as the nave of a cathedral of learning, so that

Figure 12.
Sterling Memorial
Library nave,
c. before 1960.
A. Burton Street.

the journey from the front door to the call desk past the side chapels housing the keys to information in the form of card catalogs was truly inspiring [fig. 12]. And Sterling was far from a dry textbook. Working with the architectural sculptor René Chambellan (1893–1955) and the scholar Anson Phelps Stokes (1874–1958, B.A. 1896), with whom he had collaborated on the Memorial Quadrangle, and with Andrew Keogh, Rogers made the cathedral-like library distinctly Yale's, using it to tell the University's history in a sequence of allusive, iconographically splendid spaces, embellished with genuine and invented memorabilia. If Yale's Old Library, by Austin, was a chapel, Sterling was a cathedral; Jefferson's appropriation of a Roman temple to serve as a working symbol of the university as a scholarly city of heaven on earth at the University of Virginia, America's first great research library building, was restated. Altar-like, at the end of the nave, above the call desk, Yale art professor Eugene F. Savage's (1883–1978, B.F.A. 1924) mural depicted the allegory of the female spirit of learning attended by the arts and sciences [fig. 13]. The length of the nave was lit by stained glass by G. Owen Bonawit (1891–1971) that featured famous graduates and down its center brass-trimmed glass exhibit cases displayed the University's gilded relics. The main reading room, off the transept to the left, was Gothic in its thin, taut length but pure invention in its position: it ran parallel to the main nave, constituting, in effect, a twin cathedral, devoted to research. To the right of the main entrance, a

Figure 13.
Eugene F. Savage's
Alma Mater, c. 1932.
*Sterling Memorial Library,
Yale University, Photographs
(RU 696). Manuscripts
and Archives.*

dark vestibule led to a low, cramped portal through which the light, two-story, book-lined Linonia and Brothers Reading Room, commemorating the two historic literary societies, exploded into view as a great library in an English manor house [fig. 14]. In good weather, scholars could take their books outside into a cloistered, landscaped courtyard. On the second floor, readers could enter the "Yale Library of 1742" through the doors of Reverend Samuel Russel's house in Branford, where the University's founders had met.

Typically, Rogers was not given to elaborate justifications for his stylistic choices, but in the case of Sterling Memorial Library, perhaps feeling compelled to justify his version of Goodhue's design, he made his position clear in a brief essay he wrote for the *Yale University Library Gazette* in 1928, a year after preliminary sketches of his proposal were unveiled: "The style of the new Sterling Memorial Library is as near to modern Gothic as we dared to make it. We kept, however, sufficiently close to the sound principles and tried traditions of old Gothic to be certain that there would be no sense of freakishness and no danger of becoming, in the passing of time, a little out of style."[37]

Andrew Keogh also addressed the issue of style in a not improbable leap of logic, given the connections between the Gothic Revival of the nineteenth century and the Functionalism of the 1920s then held dear by architects and historians. He stated that Modern Gothic was adopted "not only because this

Figure 14. Linonia and Brothers Reading Room, c. 1931.
Sterling Memorial Library, Yale University, Photographs (RU 696). Manuscripts and Archives.

is in keeping with the neighboring Memorial Quadrangle and with the general policy of the University, but because Gothic lends itself readily to expansion."[38] According to Keogh, the library would open with a shelf capacity of three million volumes (a significant reduction from the five million originally planned owing to the decision to diminish its size in order to ensure its quality) and seating capacity for two thousand readers at one time, but it would be so designed as to ensure almost complete flexibility—allowing for an additional one million volumes, presumably to be built in a second, smaller book stack tower, a feature never to be realized.

Rogers's claims to modernity notwithstanding, the library failed to impress William Harlan Hale (B.A. 1931), who, in an article titled "Art vs. Yale University," published in the short-lived student journal *Harkness Hoot* [fig. 15], attacked the University's ongoing program of steel-framed Gothic style buildings as "girder Gothic," a term coined by instructor Lewis P. Curtis (B.A. 1923). Hale went after the design with particular gusto, deriding as "pedantic sophistry" the choice of Gothic style for a modern university and mocking the claim that because "modern scholarship had its birth and spent its youth in Gothic buildings; therefore modern scholars should continue to work in mediaeval buildings."[39] Hale disparaged the new building "as a monument of lifelessness and decadence [that] none can surpass . . . in extravagance and falsity, . . . a great gloomy reconstruction out of a forgotten past, . . . an arch-assault upon every aesthetic conscience that must behold it. . . . Is there anything admirable in a highly functional building which

Figure 15. From "Art vs. Yale University," *Harkness Hoot*, November 15, 1930.

dresses up like a cathedral, its entrance hall a nave, its reading rooms a crossing, and its delivery desk a high altar? Is there anything remotely artistic in a vast pile whose first court is a sentimental cloister and whose second court is a Wall Street light shaft?"[40] Hale went on, concluding that: "What the Yale builders are trying to do is to deny the fact that a building must have relation to the age in which it was constructed." Hale's critical blast spread beyond New Haven. It was reprinted in *The Arts* magazine and *American Architect* and elicited the favorable responses of modernists such as Lewis Mumford (1895–1990) and Frank Lloyd Wright (1867–1959), who long had an animus for Rogers. It also led Ralph Adams Cram, Goodhue's former partner, to remark: "You seem to think that the only things of any importance are the modern things."[41]

Inspired by the library's dedication ceremony, Hale returned to the attack in April 1931, regaling the readers of *The Nation* with its stylistic irrelevance, saving the best for last, "at the end of the nave . . . a telephone booth, designed as a fourteenth-century confessional."[42] Hale found only one bright spot to the story, lauding the horizontally banded temporary wooden scaffolding that wrapped Austin's library to help in removing books to Sterling.[43] Significantly, in 1959 Hale was to change his mind when, reflecting on his earlier position while praising Eero Saarinen's new David S. Ingalls Rink (1958), he acknowledged that Yale's architecture of the past had "become authentic in the sense that any canon of taste portrays the mores and feelings of its time."[44]

Not everyone agreed with student Hale. Wilhelm Munthe, an eminent Norwegian librarian, calling the library "a combination of skyscraper, cathedral and cloister," was positively impressed: "As far as the architecture is concerned

Figure 16. Branford College library interior, c. 1930. *Residential Colleges, Yale University, Photographs (RU 632), Manuscripts and Archives.*

the Sterling Memorial Library is unique. I am not thinking of the Gothic, which is after all the dominating style at Yale and which is used in such a free, bold, pleasing, and whimsical way that it lends to the whole establishment a gay solemnity; I mean the book stack—half tower, half house. It is the first time in history that the storehouse has decided the external form. In former times one was ashamed of the storehouse and was hiding and covering it in the background. But at Yale the book skyscraper overlooks the town as a symbol that the book is a power-factor in modern society."[45]

Coincidental with Sterling's construction, the University, with funds from members of the Harkness family and the Sterling bequest, embarked on the development of ten residential colleges to house all undergraduates except freshmen in settings similar to the ones found at Oxford and Cambridge, replete with Masters' houses, dining halls, and other social spaces, as well as libraries.[46] It is beyond the scope of this essay to describe the college system or the design of the various colleges (six of which were designed in the Gothic style, the others in versions of the red brick Georgian of the original college), but it is appropriate to note that the libraries in each of the various colleges are immense assets. Two of the colleges were created as the result of renovations to the Memorial Quadrangle in 1933. In Branford College, occupying the south half of the Quadrangle, walls separating several students' suites were removed and the space was converted to form a wood-paneled library [fig. 16].[47] At the same time, to the north, Rogers planned Saybrook College with a library that retained but linked together seven student rooms located above the dining hall to form a suite of four small rooms and one large reading room with shelves adequate to hold twelve thousand books.[48] Unlike the renovation-born Branford and Saybrook colleges, Trumbull College was purpose-designed by Rogers and was in fact physically attached to the south side of Sterling Library, completing the block down to Elm Street. This college, even more than Sterling Library, exhibited a modernizing tendency within the Gothic style, although such cannot be said of its generously proportioned double-height library with its open-work wood ceiling.[49]

Jonathan Edwards College, like Saybrook and Branford, had its origin in earlier Yale buildings, the Wheelock and Dickinson dormitories (James Gamble Rogers, 1925). One of the smaller colleges, Jonathan Edwards originally included an intimately scaled library, but in 1965 the college was expanded by incorporating Weir Hall, designed by Evarts Tracy (1868–1929, B.A. 1890) and Egarton Swartwout (1870–1943, B.A. 1891). Weir Hall was initially intended as a dormitory for the senior society Skull and Bones in 1912 and completed by Everett V. Meeks (1879–1954, B.A. 1901, B.F.A. 1917, M.A. HON. 1919) in 1924, after which it was used by the School of Fine Arts. Architect Charles Brewer, Jr. (b. 1926, B. ARCH. 1949) inserted a new library, named to honor Robert A. Taft (1889–1953, B.A. 1910), a Republican senator from Ohio whose father, William H. Taft (1857–1930, B.A. 1878, L.L.D. HON. 1893), had been President during his years at Yale.

Calhoun College (1932), designed by John Russell Pope, inspired by English Gothic and Tudor precedents, includes a spacious oak-paneled, Jacobean-style library on its second floor.[50] Davenport College (James Gamble Rogers, 1933), despite its Gothic face to York Street, is designed in the American Georgian style with a library fit into the low roofs over the dining hall, as Carroll L. V. Meeks (B.A. 1928, B.F.A. 1931, M.A. 1934) put it, "in a picturesque way, permitting several secluded alcoves."[51] Next door to the south lies Pierson College (1934), also designed by Rogers in the American Georgian style, with a dramatic tower that includes a library, the two-story-high main reading room of which sits directly over the archway entrance leading to the inner courtyard.[52] In contrast to the oak paneling of most of the other college libraries, Pierson's is elaborately paneled in hand-carved natural-finish white pine. In 2005 the firm of KieranTimberlake (Stephen Kieran, b. 1951, B.A. 1973, and James Timberlake, b. 1952) added a double-height library reading room with sleek, modern, rift-sawn red oak panels articulating two levels of alcoved study space, forming a new entry to the restored original library.

The last and most elaborately detailed of the Gothic colleges to be constructed, Berkeley (1934), occupies two sites facing each other across the Cross Campus mall; in this it is unique.[53] Paul Goldberger (B.A. 1972) tells us that Rogers, searching for a way to connect the two halves of the college, "at one point came up with an extravagant plan to raise the Cross Campus approach to [Sterling] library on a viaduct-like esplanade" under which the college's library would be located "and the two Berkeley courtyards would have been connected via a cloistered walk that would pass beside the library."[54] Berkeley's library, with fireplaces at each end, linen-fold oak-paneled walls, and an elaborate plaster ceiling, holds over seven thousand books in the main reading room and a small stack room below it. An adjacent room provides for a collection of between three and four thousand additional books.

With Timothy Dwight College (1935), Rogers once again explored the American Georgian. Timothy Dwight's barrel-vaulted library was renovated in 1999 by Peter Gisolfi (b. 1946, B.A. 1966), who expanded it to three floors by excavating the crawl space, all in the style of the original but with the modern addition of a computer center.[55]

Two new residential colleges, Morse and Ezra Stiles, opened in 1963 and were designed by Eero Saarinen (1910–1961, B.F.A. 1934, M.A. HON. 1949) in a manner that reinterprets Rogers's Gothic with new construction techniques—random rubble walls impregnated with sprayed concrete—and adds to it more than a hint of medieval Italian vernacular as could be seen in the hill town of San Gimignano.[56] Each college had its own library, finished in stone, plaster, and white oak, and furnished with study tables, captain's chairs, and lounge chairs designed by Saarinen's friend and occasional collaborator Charles Eames (1907–1978). After studying the libraries in the older colleges, Saarinen determined that the best used were more intimate rather than imposing. Saarinen particularly admired Saybrook's, which, having been created out of existing bedrooms and hallways, was compartmentalized, and he followed this strategy in Stiles and Morse colleges, where the libraries consist of double-height reading rooms ringed in part by two levels of study and book alcoves. Unlike the libraries of the Rogers era, Saarinen's directly overlook the college courtyards.

Many of Yale's professional schools as well as the Graduate School are housed in purpose-built buildings, with their own classrooms, offices, and libraries. One of these, the Law School, occupies its own quadrangle (James Gamble Rogers, 1931) that also includes student housing and dining facilities. However, the Law School began in far more humble circumstances and, like the College, its origins lay in a collection of books. New Haven attorney Seth Staples (1776–1861, B.A. 1797, M.A. 1801) imported a collection of law books from England in 1800 and developed it over time, creating a library so useful to students that the Staples Law School was established around it.[57] In 1824 Staples moved to New York City and sold the law books to his partner Samuel Hitchcock. That same year, the Staples School became associated with Yale College, but the law books stayed in Hitchcock's ownership. Hitchcock died in 1845 and, because the library was integral to the school, the College purchased it in 1846 on the day the Law School became officially recognized as a department.[58]

After occupying the original Staples office on Church Street for thirty years, the Law School and its library were moved in 1850 to two rooms in the Leffingwell building next door, and then to the third floor of the new Superior Court House, designed by David R. Brown (1830–1910), in 1873 [fig. 17].[59] Accommodations for the Law School in the courthouse were likely based on the desire of members of the bar and judges to have access to the remarkable library,

Figure 17. Law School library on the third floor of the old County Court House, 165 Church Street, c. 1873–95. *Yale University Buildings and Grounds Photographs (RU 703). Manuscripts and Archives.*

which was ultimately built so that the flooring could be removed if the library outgrew its space and needed to expand to the floor below.[60] In this location, the library grew to over twelve thousand books by 1895, when it was moved to the partially completed Hendrie Hall (1894–1901).[61] This building on Elm Street, facing the Green, was designed by J. Cleveland Cady and realized in two campaigns, with the rear building constructed first and the front waiting until enough donors, including philanthropist John W. Hendrie (1821–1900, B.A. 1851, M.A. 1861), were found to fund it. With a library on the third floor of the rear building, Hendrie Hall served as the Law School from 1895 to 1931, during which time its library grew enormously, prompting development of the Sterling Law Buildings, occupying the block that confronted the Wall Street facade of the Sterling Memorial Library and the still incomplete development of what had once been called the New Campus.[62]

The principal feature of the Sterling Law Buildings is the library, the place, as Betsky has written, "where precedent is converted into current use."[63] Based directly on King's College Chapel, Cambridge, the library, designed for a collection of 250,000 books, three times the number then in Hendrie Hall, suggests what Pope's unrealized proposal for the University Library might have been like, although Rogers's scheme is less massive, not only because it is smaller but also because it is counterbalanced by the two- and three-story courtyard bounding buildings that house the classrooms, offices, and student residences composing the entire block-filling Law School quadrangle.

Figure 18. Main reading room of the law library, c. 1931. *Irvin L. Beebe.*

The main reading room [fig. 18], accommodating 266 readers, was designed with freestanding white oak bookcases arranged to form study alcoves and teak tables in different sizes that could be moved to increase reader capacity. Modern features included red and black rubber floor tiles, an elaborate ventilation system, and two elevators for pages to transport materials to readers from the seven decks of self-supporting closed book stacks. During the day, the room was lit by sunlight streaming through stained glass windows that featured medallions illustrating events and objects related to the law, and in the evenings it was lit by twenty-six circular chandeliers.

In 1970, amid campus- and citywide unrest surrounding the trial of Black Panther Bobby Seale, an arsonist set fire to the law library, destroying about five hundred books but also demonstrating the importance of the library to the school and its students, who rushed to salvage what materials they could and established a guard patrol to protect the building and collections.[64] The fire, and the virtual doubling of the Law School's student population, led to dramatic renovations. As a result, Rogers's grand reading room succumbed to a host of unfortunate interventions, including brutally scaled fluorescent pendant lights that destroyed its scale and character. In 1978 Herbert Newman (b. 1934, M.ARCH. 1959) Associates began the process of renovation and restoration, improving the law students' experience and even attracting students from other schools by replacing the long, open tables with study carrels and lounge chairs, moving noisy intrusions such as photocopiers to separate areas, removing the hanging fluorescent lighting, and installing uplighting to accentuate the elaborately painted ceiling of the main reading room, which Rogers had designed to evoke the ceiling of the Palazzo Chiaramonte at Palermo.[65] The ceiling was restored during this renovation and again in 1999, coincident with a second renovation campaign by Kallmann McKinnell and Wood Architects (KMW) (Gerhard Kallmann, b. 1915; Michael McKinnell, b. 1935; and Henry Wood, b. 1929), who, led by design principal Ted Szostkowski (b. 1947), changed the lighting once more with the installation of fixtures similar to the original chandeliers.[66] As part of this renovation, largely funded by a gift from philanthropist Lillian Goldman, for whom the library is now named, KMW gutted and rebuilt the stacks, converting two decks to study areas overlooking the reading room, and inserted an underground addition connected to the Beinecke Library. Carrels were moved from the main reading room to the stacks and replaced by tables such as had originally been in the room in an effort to recapture the "feelings of openness and sociability" that Dean Anthony Kronman (PH.D. 1972, J.D. 1975) remembered from his student days.[67]

Like the Sterling Law Buildings, but on a much more generous site, the new home to the Divinity School (1932), planned by Delano and Aldrich along the lines of Jefferson's University of Virginia, was conceived as a community within the greater whole.[68] Delano, recalling the commission in his unpublished autobiography, wrote that "the Divinity School was far removed from the main campus. I have been accused in this of copying the University of Virginia, and I am proud of it, for the University of Virginia was copied by Jefferson from the plan of Marly and that, in turn, doubtless from a Roman villa: *only* today, architects' designs spring full-fledged from the head of the designer. All this talk about 'Contemporary Architecture' seems to me like a bottle of overcharged soda water—too much gas for the water content."[69]

While Jefferson adopted the library as the principal focus of his secular university, based on a building—the Pantheon—built as a pagan temple and used in his own time as a Roman Catholic church, Delano reversed the story, placing Marquand Chapel at the commanding location that Jefferson's library enjoyed on the Virginia campus. To its south, Delano located a reading room and library separated by a robustly detailed rotunda incorporating a circular stair and a double-height, oak-paneled reading room lined on two sides with two levels of book alcoves [figs. 19–20]. Taken together, the rotunda and reading room are surely among the Yale Library system's greatest architectural assets. In 2003, after a long and complicated debate over the continued use of the Delano campus by the Divinity School, which contemplated moving to a downtown New Haven site, the partnership of Frances Halsband (b. 1943) and Robert Kliment (b. 1933, B.A. 1954, M.ARCH. 1959) completed extensive renovations that combined preservation and new interventions, including a new entry to the library, somewhat remotely located at the basement level.[70]

Figure 19. Day Missions Room, Divinity School Library, c. 2005. *Martha L. Smalley.*

Figure 20. Rotunda at the Divinity School.
Michael Marsland, Yale University.

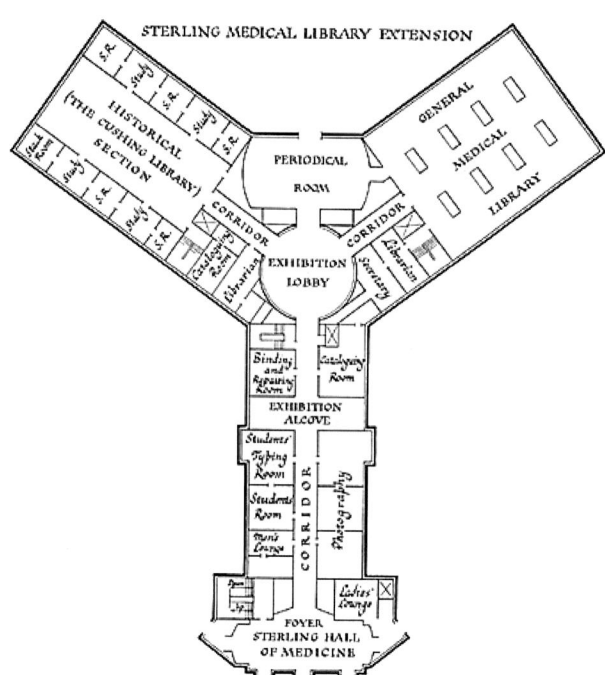

Figure 21. Grosvenor Atterbury's design for the Yale Medical Library. *Cushing/Whitney Medical Library.*

Delano and Aldrich were also responsible for the development of the new Science Hill campus, including Sage Hall (1924), home to the School of Forestry, a Gothic-style building that contained on its ground floor a twelve-thousand-volume wood-paneled, alcoved library, at the center of which was placed a gift of the alumni of the School of Forestry in East Asia: a seventeen-by-five-foot table dating from 1884, fabricated out of a single piece of mahogany.[71]

The School of Medicine, first housed on Grove Street and after 1860 mostly in converted buildings on York Street, moved in 1923 to a new complex of buildings in the Hill district south of the main campus, where some of its books were held, while the majority of medical texts were still located in Linsly-Chittenden and later Sterling Memorial Library. A new medical library (1941), designed by Grosvenor Atterbury (1869–1956, B.A. 1891), was funded by an appropriation of the Sterling Trust and built primarily as a condition of receiving the collections of Harvey Cushing (1869–1939, B.A. 1891, M.A. HON. 1913, SC.D. HON. 1919), Arnold C. Klebs (1870–1943), and John F. Fulton (1899–1960), who among them had accumulated one of the strongest medical historical libraries in the world.[72] Other collectors followed suit, including Edward Streeter (1874–1947, B.A. 1898), who contributed his collection of ancient weights and measures. Atterbury, Cushing's friend and classmate, worked on plans for the library for four years, ultimately proposing a Y-shaped design [fig. 21] extending from the Sterling Hall of Medicine (Charles Z. Klauder [1872–1938], 1924) that split the historical and general collections into two wings housing a total of

Figure 22. Memorial Rotunda, Cushing/Whitney Medical Library. *Michael Marsland, Yale University.*

Figure 23. Medical Historical Library, 2005. *Terry Dagradi, Yale University.*

about four hundred thousand books, joined by a rotunda, a spectacularly elegant room memorializing Harvey Cushing, ringed by a balcony, executed in blue sheet plastic walls trimmed with aluminum [fig. 22], combining the traditional classicism of Klauder's School of Medicine with what was for Yale a startling modernity. Klebs admired Atterbury's plans for the double-height historical wing, a distinctly traditional wood-paneled and wood-beamed room [fig. 23], noting that "a long hall with a balcony, the walls covered by books, is just what one wants, the aesthetic background for comparative and individual work that will take place in the center. Two floors of alternating study and stack rooms, all accessible from the balcony in the second floor though definitely private and undisturbed by casual wanderers and curiosity seekers, who can find a welcome below."[73] This arrangement also included a large fireplace and oak woodwork, while the more functional, bare-bones, even utilitarian balconied general library wing had long work tables and study alcoves.

The space conceived in the late 1930s was no longer sufficient for the School of Medicine by the 1980s, when an increase in materials and patrons, as well as changes in the ways that collections were made available electronically, necessitated additions and renovations carried out in 1990 by Allan Dehar (b. 1936) and Alexander Purves (b. 1935, B.A. 1958, M.ARCH. 1965) with funds from Harvey Cushing's daughter Betsy Cushing Whitney (1908–1998).[74] Great care was taken to match new materials to the old, from the exterior brick cladding to the floor tiles and cypress wood paneling of the corridors. Supplementary storage and conservation space for the historical collections were added, along with a new, dramatically skylit central information room in a semicircular addition between the preexisting wings, and the name was changed to the Harvey Cushing/John Hay Whitney Medical Library.

Yale's great expansion of the 1920s and 1930s came to a close with America's entrance into the Second World War in 1941. After the war, the University's building program was slow to recover lost momentum for many reasons, not the least of which was depleted funds. But, under the leadership of A. Whitney Griswold (1906–1963, B.A. 1929, PH.D. 1933), Yale's first president appointed in the postwar era, who served from 1950 to his death, the University began once again to build, realizing some notable buildings that reflected the stylistic modernism that Rogers and especially Delano held in disdain. Three of the buildings realized under Griswold were significant libraries, most notably the Beinecke Rare Book and Manuscript Library (1963) designed by Gordon F. Bunshaft (1909–1990), a principal design partner of the firm of Skidmore, Owings and Merrill. Now regarded as one of Yale's architectural showpieces and a masterpiece of mid-twentieth-century modernist architecture, the Beinecke was initially greeted with considerable skepticism by students and faculty who variously questioned its abstract massing and detail amid its Gothic and Classical neighbors, and who saw it as too much: "a showman's building," to use the phrase Nicholas Adams applied to it in his recent history of the Skidmore firm. "As a

Figure 24. Beinecke Plaza, 1963. *Ezra Stoller © Esto*.

dazzling evocation of abstract painting in the form of geology," Adams wrote, "it is a unique experiment, both loved and despised."⁷⁵ To Vincent Scully (b. 1920, B.A. 1940, PH.D. 1949), surveying "architecture and man at Yale" in a 1964 article published in the *Saturday Review*, the Beinecke reflected "no sense of its relationship to men, because its conception was so abstract."⁷⁶

The Beinecke is only the fourth of Yale's libraries to be housed in a single-purpose, freestanding building—the three previous being the Old Library, Sterling Memorial Library, and the Day Missions Library (of which more below). The decision to construct a new library exclusively for rare books was undertaken at the urging of University Librarian James Babb (1899–1968, B.A. 1925, M.A. HON. 1945), who protested not only the lack of space for growth in Sterling's Rare Book Room but also the fact that the lack of proper climate control was taking a toll on the collection. Located on the southwest corner of the Hewitt Quadrangle, now unofficially called Beinecke Plaza, Beinecke Library completed Thomas Hastings's sixty-year-old Bicentennial concept of a monumental core on what was once called the New Campus [fig. 24]. The building was the gift of three brothers, Edwin J. (1886–1970, B.A. 1907), Frederick W. (1887–1971, B.PHIL. 1909), and Walter (1888–1958, B.A. 1910) Beinecke, all bibliophiles with

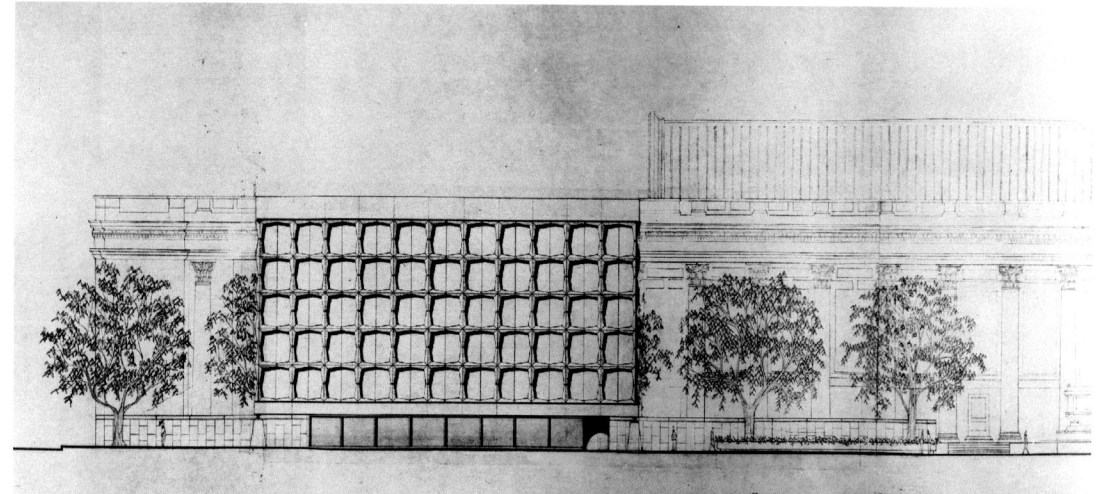

Figure 25. Elevation drawing of the Beinecke Library by Gordon Bunshaft, 1963. *Photographs of the Beinecke Rare Book and Manuscript Library, Yale University, 1961–1963. Manuscripts and Archives.*

diverse business interests, including building construction and S & H Green Stamps.

Various architects were considered for a competition to pick the new library's designer, including Edward Durell Stone (1902–1978) and Robert O'Connor (1895–1993), the latter a mediocre designer but a library specialist. Significantly, Edwin J. Beinecke, a former chairman of the George A. Fuller Construction Company, expressly wished that Eero Saarinen not compete because of his reputation for cost overruns, a reputation University President Griswold agreed was deserved. Paul Rudolph (1918–1997), Chair of the Department of Architecture, claimed to have advocated Ludwig Mies van der Rohe (1886–1969) for the job — and Mies spent part of the fall 1959 term as visiting professor in the department, perhaps with the hope of cementing the deal. Mies may or may not have been asked to compete; Bunshaft was and declined to do so. As a result, no competition was held, and Bunshaft was chosen, probably with the expectation that he would deliver a Mies-inspired glass box (Skidmore, Owings and Merrill was so much influenced by Mies in those days that it was waggishly called "Three Blind Mies"). And truth to tell, Bunshaft's design [fig. 25] owes a great deal to Mies' work, especially his unrealized project for the convention center in Chicago (1953–54).[77] But the design was very much its own thing, and as time has shown, a brilliant interpretation of both the classicism of the Bicentennial buildings and the Gothicism of the Sterling Law Buildings that together form its site context.

Beinecke has attracted wide attention since its completion, when virtually all were dazzled by the idea of housing one of the great collections of rare books in the world in a 50-foot-tall, 35-by-60-foot dark plate-glass-sheathed tower holding about 160,000 books, set at the core of a grand, double-height, cathedral-like, 86-foot-wide, 130-foot-long, and 58-foot tall exhibition hall, raised one floor above street level, and beautifully, even mysteriously bathed in dim natural light coming through a regular pattern of translucent Vermont Danby marble

Figure 26. The Beinecke Library stack tower and interior. *Ezra Stoller © Esto*.

Figure 27. Beinecke courtyard with Isamu Noguchi's Sun, Chance, and Earth.
Ezra Stoller © Esto.

Figure 28. Periodical reading room of the Art + Architecture Library, 1963.
Ezra Stoller © Esto.

panels set between a structural frame [fig. 26]. That frame, a Vierendeel or square truss, formed of steel sheathed in blue-gray granite and conveying in its details some of the intricacy of the Gothic, was supported only at the corners [frontispiece], a structural feat of some consequence allowing the treasure box–like building to be lifted above the expansive granite-paved plaza that is also the roof of an underground portion of the library serving as the scholar's world of reading and seminar rooms and faculty and curatorial offices. This underground world draws its own natural light from a sunken court east of the building that in turn has as its focus a group of Isamu Noguchi's (1904–1988) specially commissioned geometrically determined marble sculptures representing Sun, Chance, and Earth [fig. 27].

Completed at a time when the heroic scale of structurally exhibitionistic modernism was being challenged by a new generation of student architects, the building was a target of protests, in part because the once casual Hewitt Quadrangle had been reorganized as a highly stylized plaza reminiscent to some, including Yale's preeminent architectural historian Vincent Scully, of the blindingly bright, desolate spaces depicted in the 1920s paintings of Giorgio de Chirico (1888–1978). But even the once hostile Scully, writing in 2004, has partially come to terms with the "frigid perfection" of the Beinecke: "There it is on the empty plaza that was sterilized . . . as perfect as a table radio and conveying no more sense of architectural scale. . . . It is a sterile setting, but one has to admit that the building is impressive, if heavily theatrical, inside. The books enshrined in the center, the unearthly light, the height to the roof, all create another dream landscape, but here a more richly emotional one" than in the surrealist plaza.[78]

Figure 29. The Art + Architecture Library's north-facing reading room, 1963.
Ezra Stoller © Esto.

Figure 30. The east-facing reading room of the Art + Architecture Library, 1963.
Ezra Stoller © Esto.

The second most celebrated—and derided—building of the Griswold era was Paul Rudolph's Art + Architecture Building (1963). Although reams have been written about the building, very little has been said about one of its most important features, the Arts Library.[79] Occupying the entire ground floor, the 150-seat library, housing approximately half of Yale's 120,000 books covering the various visual arts as well as city planning, consisted of three reading rooms wrapping the stacks [figs. 28–30]. The room on the south, except for a strategically located corner window, was protected from the stares of pedestrians on Chapel Street by a high wall forming a moat that also let light into basement-level courts and studios and, via ingeniously designed monitors, into sub-basement studios as well. To the north the library overlooked a similarly organized but more spaciously proportioned sunken courtyard. But the library's glory was its soaring double-height, east-facing reading room with minstrel balcony. Configured and proportioned much like many of the residential college dining halls, this room was lit by large clerestory windows on the east, while on the west similarly proportioned windows provided visual connection with the building's second-floor exhibition gallery. A lower bay, opening off the side, provided a more intimate area—a "cave" to contrast with the "goldfish bowl" of the main reading room—the terms being those Rudolph used frequently to express his belief that basic human moods could be architecturally addressed with juxtaposed spaces of compression and release. As with the rest of the building, the library's wall surfaces consisted largely of hand-chiseled, buff-colored, ribbed concrete, reflecting the influence on Rudolph of Kenzo Tange's Administration Building of the Kagawa Prefecture in Takamatsu, Japan (1958), and the floors were carpeted in bright orange that gave the concrete a warm, almost rosy, glow. Rudolph designed the furniture as well, consisting of built-in De Stijl–inspired, vermillion-painted, refectory-like work tables topped by slablike, shiny white Formica writing surfaces. The vertiginous minstrel balcony, accessible by an open staircase, held Rudolph-designed pinwheel-planned study carrels intended specifically for graduate students in the history of art.

To Walter McQuade, the library's twenty-foot-high main reading room exhibited "more repose" than most of the other large rooms in the building.[80] Vincent Scully also deemed the Arts Library "one of the most successful spaces in the building: well lighted, expansive where it needs to be, offering a multitude of vistas that continue outward toward the street and the courts, and upward through the building and toward the sky."[81]

Although the Arts Library was itself a considerable success, the path leading to it was not, leading Jules Prown (b. 1930), founding Director of the Yale British Art Center, to claim that the fact that "the architect was his own client" eliminated "a critical corrective . . . from the architectural process," resulting in a trivialization of the library in what was "primarily an art and architecture school." Prown regarded as "reasonable" the decision to have a grand staircase lead to the building's main entrance on the second floor, but considered the failure to cel-

Figure 31. York Street entrance to the Art + Architecture Library, 1963. *Ezra Stoller © Esto*.

ebrate the street-level entrance to the library a form of "petty-mindedness [that] would not have survived unchallenged in a reasonable interchange between client and architect."[82] Rudolph's intent to make the library's direct street entrance little more than a mouse hole [fig. 31] was, as Prown points out, deliberate, citing the architect's statement that the Art + Architecture Building was conceived "for the people who are going to *make* things.... It is not so much for people using the library. They are temperamentally very, very different. Everybody who is going to that library learns how you get in."[83]

Although the library was not damaged in the 1969 fire that swept through the Art + Architecture Building's top four floors, its appearance was severely compromised, along with that of the rest of the building, when in 1974 the hung, sprayed asbestos ceilings crucial to its design were ripped out after they were determined to be the cause of an eye infection developed by arts librarian Robert C. Kaufmann (1937–2009). From then until the restoration of 2008, the library, like the rest of the building, had only the underside of the structural concrete slabs to serve as ceilings, with bright but harsh fluorescent lights replacing the exposed warm-toned incandescent bulbs that Rudolph, working with lighting designer Richard Kelly (1910–1977, B.ARCH. 1944), had placed in continuous troughs between the structural beams and the asbestos-covered ceiling plenums.

In 2008 the Art + Architecture Building was restored with a gift from Sid R.

Bass (b. 1942, B.A. 1965), who asked that it be renamed Rudolph Hall in honor of its recently deceased architect, whose reputation had been sadly besmirched partially as a result of the fire and the asbestos problem.[84] The renovation was the work of Charles Gwathmey (1938–2009, M.ARCH. 1962), who was also given responsibility for the design of the Jeffrey H. Loria (b. 1940, B.A. 1962) Center for the History of Art that was built on the adjoining site to the Art + Architecture Building's north, where a small tenement and a single-family residence long since converted to commercial use had stood. Gwathmey's restoration of Rudolph's building included the reinstallation of ceiling plenums using a sophisticated new climate-control system and new lighting designed by Robert Leiter (b. 1963) that recaptures the spirit of the original by replicating the incandescent bulbs as energy-efficient fixtures.

Rudolph Hall and Loria are connected at every level, permitting the library's expansion into the new building on both the first floor and the basement level. The expanded library, now known as the Robert B. Haas (b. 1947, B.A. 1969) Family Arts Library, serves students and faculty in the Schools of Drama, Art, and Architecture, as well as the Department of the History of Art and the Yale University Art Gallery. Gwathmey replaced the former north court of Rudolph's building with a dramatic top-lit reading room inspired by two memorable interiors designed by the Finnish architect Alvar Aalto (1898–1976): his library at Viipuri, Finland (1927–1935), and the dining room at his Baker House dormitory at the Massachusetts Institute of Technology (1948). In contrast to Rudolph's original cramped library entry, the new room in the Haas Library, essentially an enclosed courtyard between Rudolph and Loria, is easily entered from a generous lobby on the first floor through spacious doors leading past the library's circulation desk to a dramatic stair that takes readers down to a double-height seating area on the building's basement level [fig. 32]. Opening off this enclosed reading court is the William H. Wright (b. 1960, B.A. 1982) Special Collections Exhibition Area, where students may work with rare materials from the Arts of the Book, art and architecture, and drama collections. The combined facility of the Haas Library, occupying space in Loria and Rudolph, now has a capacity of about 125,000 volumes. A new internal elevator meets the guidelines set by the Americans with Disabilities Act and facilitates the efficient movement of books between the library's two floors. Gwathmey's restoration of Rudolph Hall has brought that building's portion of the library back to its former glory so that now the Haas Library as a whole can easily be ranked as one of Yale's library gems.

The brutalism of the Art + Architecture Building was stiffened and abstracted in the slablike Becton Engineering and Applied Science Center (Marcel Breuer [1902–1981] and Hamilton Smith [b. 1925, M.ARCH. 1950], 1970) overlooking Grove Street Cemetery, where it replaced Winchester and North Sheffield halls (J. Cleveland Cady, 1892 and 1873), two of three similarly scaled nineteenth-century buildings that formed a coherent but varied streetscape.[85] Becton's accor-

Figure 32. View of the Hass Family Arts Library's lower level. *Michael Marsland, Yale University.*

dionlike pre-cast concrete facade, incorporating pipes and ducts rather than windows in its folds, is lifted on massive sculpted pilotis, forming an arcade along Prospect Street behind which lies a blandly detailed, balconied reading room.

Beinecke was Yale's first library to incorporate a significant underground component. The second was the Kline Science Library, as part of a complex at the top of Hillhouse Avenue designed by Philip Johnson (1906–2005, D.F.A. HON. 1978) and completed in 1965.[86] The two-story, twenty-five-thousand-square-foot library is entered from the lobby of the Kline Biology Tower, where a bridge and staircase lead down to stacks and a reading room that seats about ninety readers at long walnut tables with cantilever chairs designed by Marcel Breuer. The reading room is separated from the reference area by glazed brick columns that pierce down into the library from the facade, and it opens onto a light court cut into the quadrangle containing a sculpture by Raoul Ubac (1910–1985).

The third, and far and away the most controversial of Yale's underground libraries, was the Cross Campus Library (1971), designed by Edward Larrabee Barnes (1915–2004), who served as master planner for the University from 1968 to 1971.[87] Though intensely used, it was never a popular favorite. In fact, from the moment the project was announced by the University in spring 1968— when it was proposed as a home to collections in Slavic languages—the Cross

Figure 33. The Cross Campus Library, c. mid-1970s. *Ysidro R. Barron*.

Campus Library (CCL) was the subject of intense criticism, especially among students, who attacked not only the facility but also what, in an era intent on participatory democracy, they regarded as the University's high-handed, top-down decision-making processes.[88] CCL [fig. 33] was eventually realized as an extension of Sterling Memorial Library, functioning as an undergraduate library accommodating course reserves and a broad selection of most-in-demand volumes, thereby relieving pressure on overcrowded reading rooms in Sterling. A new staircase cut into the center of Sterling's nave connected to a tunnel under High Street and led to the new library under the broad Cross Campus mall where four thirty-by-thirty-two-foot sunken light courts, one at each corner, provided natural light to the upper floor of the two-level facility. The route between Sterling and CCL passed through a lounge seating 176 people and providing locker space as well as an area for vending machines dispensing soft drinks and snacks, the number of which grew to such an extent that the area became known as "Machine City." The 223-by-140-foot, 750-seat library opened with 50,000 volumes chosen on the basis of consultation with the faculty and computer analysis of 270,000 call slips for books taken out in 1968–69. By 1975–76, CCL's collection had grown to 122,580 "intensive-use" volumes.

Protests led by Bradley Nitkin (1947–2009, B.A. 1969) against early plans that called for a grid of skylights poking through and compromising the recreational utility of the Cross Campus mall resulted in a less intrusive but fundamentally soulless environment that seemed worlds apart from that in Sterling Library. As Patrick Pinnell put it: to walk from CCL's "space-odyssey plastic laminate to Sterling's stone-paved nave" was "frankly surreal," contrasting two different meanings about "what it means to learn. On one end, knowledge . . . seemingly understood as information, on the other . . . as religion."[89]

Figure 34. Anne T. and Robert M. Bass Library. *Michael Marsland, Yale University*.

CCL suffered major structural problems from the very start, especially leaking roofs that defied attempts at repair. In 2006 the much-used but little-loved facility was closed and completely rebuilt, reopening in October 2007 as the Anne T. (b. 1948) and Robert M. Bass (b. 1948, B.A. 1971) Library [fig. 34].[90] The transformation was astonishing. As redesigned by Thomas Beeby (b. 1941, M.ARCH. 1965), Bass emerged as one of Yale's most inviting libraries. Beeby replaced the intrusive stair in the middle of Sterling's nave with a circular stair to one side located in space formerly occupied by card catalog cabinets. Machine City was transformed into an elegantly furnished, quiet reading room named to honor donor William H. Wright II, while the four light courts of the original CCL were retained, but an intrusive ventilation pavilion was removed. The after-hours entrance was moved to the east end of the library, where a Gothic-style pavilion in the manner of Rogers was constructed, providing a new stair and elevator down from the Cross Campus mall to the Thain Family Café. Beyond the café, the two-level reading room was finished, not in the plain-vanilla, white sheetrock, plastic, and aluminum of CCL but in meticulously detailed stone, brick, wood, and mullioned glass exemplifying Rogers's sense of Modern Gothic. "If Sterling is the cathedral of reading," Beeby stated, "this is the crypt."[91]

While the underground expansion of Sterling Library in the form of CCL proved at best a mixed blessing, the decision to locate the Irving S. Gilmore (1900–1986, B.A. 1923) Music Library (1998) in a former light court—the one William Harlan Hale had deemed a "Wall Street light shaft"—proved an unqualified success [fig. 35]. As designed by Shepley Bulfinch Richardson and Abbott, architects charged with the renovation and restoration of much of Sterling Memorial Library in the 1990s, the Gilmore Library sits under soaring, pleasantly theatrical Gothic-inspired arches that support a vaulted roof sixty-five feet

Figure 35.
Irving S. Gilmore
Music Library.
Peter Aaron
© *Esto*.

above a two-level facility for reading and listening, with stacks, carrels, and a sound recording room located in a new basement underneath the courtyard.[92]

With the construction of the British Art Center (BAC), designed by Louis I. Kahn (1901–1974, D.F.A. HON. 1965) and funded by Paul Mellon (1907–1999, B.A. 1929, L.H.D. HON. 1967), the University returned to the more traditional conception of a library as a light-filled ennobling place of research.[93] The BAC, Kahn's last great building, was completed by former associates Anthony Pellecchia (b. 1940) and Marshall Meyers (1931–2001, M.ARCH. 1957) in 1977, three years after the architect's death. Kahn had been impressed by the rare book library at Mellon's "Brick House" in Virginia—a 1940 Georgian design by William Adams Delano—and for him, as the BAC's first Director, Jules Prown reports, the British Art Center, "despite its considerable amount of gallery and teaching space," was "first and foremost a library."[94] Kahn had hoped that the BAC would fill the entire Chapel Street block from High to York Streets, but when it became clear that the Calvary Baptist Church (Rufus G. Russell [1823–1896], 1871) at the York Street corner would not be torn down, Kahn consoled himself with the prospect that the church would eventually give way to a freestanding arts library that he even prepared preliminary sketches for—something that did not occur, with library expansion taking place in 2008 in the renewed Rudolph Hall and the new Loria Center for the History of Art.

Figure 36.
Yale Center for
British Art Library.
*Richard Caspole, Yale
Center for British Art.*

As realized, the BAC library occupies a prominent location on the building's second floor, its south-facing, double-height reading room, with bow-back chairs and simple oak tables lit by suspended stainless-steel illuminated drums designed by Richard Kelly, overlooked by a balcony containing stacks [fig. 36]. The library opens off a glorious three-story white oak–paneled skylit room designated Library Court. In keeping with the building as a whole, the library is austere, but it is nonetheless, as Duncan Robinson (M.A. 1967), Director of the BAC between 1981 and 1995, has written, rich in details such as the paneled stairs in the stacks, "almost as secretive as the hidden stairs to some manorial priest's hole." It repeats, Robinson notes, "on a miniature scale" the "initial embrace" of the building's entrance court, "welcoming, reassuring, and whispering of hidden treasures. A private echo of the original, public statement."[95] Vincent Scully places Kahn's library firmly in the traditions of English libraries and consequently those by Rogers for Yale. In the library, Scully writes, the building's system of regular, concrete framed bays can be "seen at its best in defining a calm and articulated spread of space, and the sun pours in through the big windows to light the blond oak of the fittings and the warm bindings of the books on the shelves. It is an English library right enough, with all the sheltered, sunbeam-moted peace of the originals, evoked by very simple means. Yale has not seen anything like it since James Gamble Rogers, even though its space is also notable by the passage through it of enormous, silvery, cylindrical ducts, worthy of High Tech's shiniest fantasies."[96]

The impact of Kahn's British Art Center can be seen in the design of the fifth of Yale's stand-alone libraries, Seeley G. Mudd (1983), the work of Harold Roth (b. 1934, M.ARCH. 1957) and William F. Moore (b. 1941, B.A. 1963, M.ARCH. 1966) [figs. 37–38]. It was built to house government documents that can be consulted by the public and to store overflow of the 1.6 million books in Yale's other libraries.[97] More warehouse than reading room, the design of Mudd pays homage not only to the work of Kahn but also to J. Cleveland Cady's straightforward buildings for the Sheffield Scientific School on Prospect Street, the last remaining one of which, the Sheffield Chemical Laboratory, was renovated by Roth and Moore in 1985 and renamed Watson Hall. Mudd's exposed reinforced concrete frame infilled with water-struck brick laid in Flemish bond, and trimmed in carved buff limestone, does much to provide visual relief to what is essentially a blank-faced warehouse. Inside a four-story-high court, diffused clerestory light floods into the main control area and adjacent lounge. The building, sited in a comparatively remote corner of the campus, on Mansfield Street between the right-of-way of what had once been the Farmington Canal and Sachem Street, is slated to give way to the two proposed new residential colleges.

The Lewis Walpole Library, one of Yale's highly specialized libraries, is also its most unusually situated, located in the Cowles-Lewis House (1782–84) in Farmington, Connecticut, outside Hartford, former home to Wilmarth Sheldon Lewis (1895–1979, B.A. 1918, L.L.D. HON. 1965) and his wife, Annie Burr Lewis (1902–1959). Soon after his graduation, Lewis began amassing what would become the definitive collection of letters and other papers, books, and possessions pertaining to Horace Walpole (1717–1797), the English writer and man of letters whose twenty-seven-year career in Parliament is said to have been without significant political influence but whose writing provides a brilliant mirror of social life in the late eighteenth century. Walpole's novel *The Castle of Otranto* was the first Gothic romance, and his house, Strawberry Hill, on the Thames River at Twickenham, west of London, was one of the first examples of the Gothic revival in architecture.[98]

In 1928, shortly after purchasing the Cowles House, Lewis retained William Adams Delano to adapt it to modern family life and to add a library, executed in what the English critic John Cornforth described as Lutyens-esque "Wrennaissance" consisting of a one-and-a-half-story gabled volume with oculi on the long side at the upper level and a tall round-headed window at the pedimented end [fig. 39].[99] The new library was conceived as a setting for conversation, not for scholarly research. But as the collection grew, Richard Kimball (1899–1997, B.A. 1922, B.F.A. 1927) added a fireproof storage facility in 1934, and in 1953 the squash court was converted to use as a print room. The library was added on to again in 1965. At that time there were twenty-three thousand books in the collection, which together with the house were given to Yale upon Lewis's death in 1979.

Figure 37. Mudd Library exterior. © *1983 Steve Rosenthal for Roth and Moore Architects. Used with permission.*

Figure 38. Mudd Library foyer. © *1983 Steve Rosenthal for Roth and Moore Architects. Used with permission.*

Figure 39. The Lewis Walpole Library from the west lawn before the
2006–07 renovation project. *Lewis Walpole Library.*

In 2006, plans were developed by Mark Simon (b. 1946, M.ARCH. 1972) of Centerbrook Architects, providing new climate controls, accessibility for disabled scholars, and additional workspace in a new asymmetrically massed, metal-roofed, barnlike building containing a mezzanine-level reading room lit by a continuous shed dormer.[100]

The Elizabethan Club houses what is probably Yale's most unusual library — and certainly one of its most exclusive. It is stored in a vault in a Federal-style house on College Street built around 1775, where members of the club may use the collection of about three hundred volumes of sixteenth- and seventeenth-century literature [fig. 40].[101] The house was purchased and endowed to the University by Alexander Smith Cochran (1874–1929, B.A. 1896), who established a club in 1911 to hold his collection of Elizabethan books and promote conversation about literature and art among undergraduates. The materials are also available to other scholars at the Beinecke, where they may be brought upon request. In 1995–96 the house and its garden were restored by architect Kenneth Boroson (b. 1954, M.ARCH. 1984), and a new sunroom and covered porch created more space for club members.[102]

Remarkably, almost all of Yale's purpose-built libraries have survived the vicissitudes of time, with the exception of the Cross Campus Library and the Day Missions Library (1911–13), designed by Delano and Aldrich as part of the first Divinity School campus, located on the block bounded by Elm, College, High, and Wall Streets.[103] Set between East and West Divinity Halls (Richard Morris Hunt [1827–1895], 1870), to which it was connected, the Gothic-style library consisted of a ground floor providing for five faculty as well as seminar and reference rooms, and on the second floor, a tall, approximately thirty-by-sixty-foot book-lined reading room lit by generously sized windows [figs. 41–42].

Figure 40. Elizabethan Club, 1986. *T. Charles Erickson*.

The five-bay buttressed exterior stood in sharp contrast to the decidedly French mansarded buildings by Richard Morris Hunt that were connected at their south end, along Elm Street, by the Battell Chapel (Russell Sturgis, Jr. [1836–1909], 1876) and the Trowbridge Library (1881), probably also designed by Hunt in collaboration with his associate Edward E. Raht (1844–?).[104] This was an imposing, book-lined, high-ceilinged, ground-floor room, ringed by a balcony, with a dramatically shaped arrangement of upper walls and ceiling seemingly paneled in horizontally laid beaded boarding. In 1931 Trowbridge and the Day Missions Library—each a treasure—fell to the wrecker's ball when the Divinity School moved to its new campus and its central campus site was redeveloped as Calhoun College.

So this overview brings us to the present situation. Despite the growth of electronic retrieval of information, new libraries will be undertaken as the University expands its programs and facilities, providing up-to-date access to both printed and electronic media. Each of the two new residential colleges, for which I am privileged to be given design responsibility, will have its own library; the consolidated home of the School of Management designed by Norman Foster (b. 1935, M.ARCH. 1962, D.F.A. HON. 2003) in association with Gruzen Samton (Jordan Gruzen, b. 1934, and Peter Samton, b. 1935) will have a splendid reading room overlooking Whitney Avenue at the termination of Sachem Street. While a plan for a second book tower at Sterling Library was said to have been considered by Rogers, such is no longer contemplated. Instead, and from the point of view of architectural art, the storage problem for less frequently consulted titles, as well as for the collections of the Art Gallery and the British Art Center, is being met in the Library Shelving Facility (Bruce Scott, b. 1937, Russell Scott Steedle and Capone, 1998), a highly serviceable, modular facility—the ultimate

Figure 41. Exterior of the Day Missions Library, before 1931. *Yale University Buildings and Grounds Photographs (RU 703). Manuscripts and Archives.*

Figure 42. Interior of the Day Missions Library, before 1931. *Yale University Buildings and Grounds Photographs (RU 703). Manuscripts and Archives.*

Figure 43. Library Shelving Facility, 1998. *Danuta A. Nitecki.*

closed stack, not as a tower such as at Sterling, but in a horizontal configuration easily navigable by professionals who respond to readers' requests with amazing efficiency, delivering books to the campus on very short notice [fig. 43].

As this is being written, the University is confronting serious budgetary challenges attributable to the downturn in the global economy, but all of us who care about libraries—the collections and the facilities necessary to their dissemination and preservation—can take comfort in the past fifteen years of exceptional stewardship of University facilities that has resulted in an extraordinary program of renewal and expansion. And one can but hope that with the return of greater prosperity, Yale's heritage of libraries will continue to be honored and extended.

One last thought: Yale's libraries have been designed to meet reasonable performance standards, but just as important, perhaps even more important, they have been designed to foster a sense of pleasure in learning. Like so much of Yale's architecture, the libraries transcend the utilitarian to reach a higher plane of environmentalism, emblematizing learning as the great obligation and pleasure of civilized life.

NOTES

1. I wish to thank Sarah Acheson for her extraordinary assistance in the research and preparation of this essay and to others who helped me with this project, including Yale librarians and archivists Toby Appel, Jason Eiseman, Amy Limpitlaw, Cynthia Ostroff, Judith Schiff, Laura Tatum, and Allan Townsend. A number of architects have also been very generous with their time, and I wish to thank them as well: Ken Boroson, Allan Dehar, Peter Gisolfi, Michael Maza of Kliment Halsband, Alexander Purves, Michele Silvetti-Schmitt of Hammond Beeby Rupert Ainge, Ted Szostkowski of Kallmann, McKinnell and Wood, Centerbrook Architects Manager of Public Relations Genie Devine, and Carin Whitney, Communications Manager at KieranTimberlake.

For the early history of Yale and its library, see Joshua L. Chamberlain, ed. *Yale University: Its History, Influence, Equipment, and Characteristics* (Boston: N. Nerndon, 1900); Anthony N. B. Garvan, *Architecture and Town Planning in Colonial Connecticut* (New Haven, CT: Yale University Press, 1951), 145–49; Brooks Mather Kelley, *Yale: A History* (New Haven, CT: Yale University Press, 1974); George Wilson Pierson, *The Founding of Yale: The Legend of the Forty Folios* (New Haven, CT: Yale University Press, 1988); James E. Mooney, "Yale and Her Early Books," *Yale University Library Gazette* 77, no. 1/2 (2002): 39–50. For additional information on Yale's libraries, see John Jorg Boll, "Library Architecture 1800–1875," PH.D. thesis, University of Illinois, 1961, 161–98; Anthony Hobson, *Great Libraries* (London: Weidenfeld and Nicholson, 1970), 222–33; Merrily A. Taylor, *The Yale University Library, 1701–1978: Its History, Collections, and Present Organization* (New Haven, CT: Yale University Library, 1978); Thomas Frederick O'Connor, "The Yale University Library, 1865–1931," PH.D. dissertation, Columbia University, 1984; Judith Schiff, "Yale University Library," in David H. Stam, ed., *International Dictionary of Library Histories* (Chicago: Fitzroy Dearborn, 2001), 939–44.

2. For Yale's buildings and campus history, see Montgomery Schuyler, "Architecture of American Colleges II—Yale," *Architectural Record* 26, no. 6 (1909): 393–416; Reuben A. Holden, *Yale: A Pictorial History* (New Haven, CT: Yale University Press, 1967); George W. Pierson, *Yale: A Short History* (New Haven, CT: Yale University, 1976); Richard C. Carroll, ed., *Buildings and Grounds of Yale University* (New Haven, CT: Yale University Press, 1979). Essential to Yale's architectural history and that of its host city are Elizabeth Mills Brown, *New Haven: A Guide to Its Architecture and Urban Design* (New Haven, CT: Yale University Press, 1976); Patrick L. Pinnell, *Yale University: The Campus Guide* (New York: Princeton Architectural Press, 1999); Vincent Scully, Catherine Lynn, Eric Vogt, and Paul Goldberger, *Yale in New Haven: Architecture and Urbanism* (New Haven, CT: Yale University, 2004). For the development of Yale's campus in relationship

to that of other American colleges and universities, see Paul Venable Turner, *Campus: An American Planning Tradition* (Cambridge, MA: MIT Press, 1984).

3. Norman M. Isham, "The Original College House at Yale," *Yale Alumni Weekly*, October 20, 1916, pp. 114–20; Andrew Keogh, "The Yale Library of 1742," in Harry Miller Lydenberg and Andrew Keogh, eds., *William Warner Bishop: A Tribute* (New Haven, CT: Yale University Press, 1941), 76–87; Garvan, *Architecture and Town Planning*, 146–47.

4. Turner, *Campus*, 38–46; Eric Vogt, "Cultivating Types: The Rise and Fall of the Brick Row," in Scully et al., *Yale in New Haven*, 72–74.

5. James F. O'Gorman, *Henry Austin: In Every Variety of Architectural Style* (Middletown, CT: Wesleyan University Press, 2008), 125–27. Town's involvement is also discussed in Boll, "Library Architecture," 175–76. For more on Austin's College Library, see Chamberlain, *Yale University*, 192–94; Holden, *Yale*; Brown, *New Haven*, 123; Taylor, *Yale University Library*, 9–11; O'Connor, "Yale University Library," 23–25; Pinnell, *Yale University*, 14–17. Vogt, "Cultivating Types," 88–89.

6. O'Gorman, *Henry Austin*, 126.

7. Ibid., 128. For Austin's early work, see pages 7–23.

8. Ezekiel Porter Belden, *Sketches of Yale College* (New York: Saxton & Miles, 1843), 98. Quoted in Vogt, "Cultivating Types," 89.

9. Pinnell, *Yale University*, 14–15.

10. Lyman Hotchkiss Bagg, *Four Years at Yale* (New Haven, CT: Chatfield, 1871), 21. Quoted in Holden, *Yale*.

11. Brown, *New Haven*, 123.

12. George C. Holt, "A General Grumble," *Yale Literary Magazine* 31, no. 2 (1865): 72. Quoted in Catherine Lynn, "Building Yale and Razing It from the Civil War to the Great Depression," in Scully et al., *Yale in New Haven*, 109.

13. Lynn, "Building Yale," 109.

14. Kathleen A. Curran, *A Forgotten Architect of the Gilded Age: Josiah Cleaveland Cady's Legacy* (Hartford: Watkinson Library and Department of Fine Arts, Trinity College, 1993), 30–34. For more on Chittenden Hall, see "The Old Yale and the New," *New York Times,* April 19, 1896, p. 25; Montgomery Schuyler, "The Works of Cady, Berg and See," *Architectural Record* 6, no. 4 (1897): 517–53. Chamberlain, *Yale University*, 108–9, 195–96; *Report of the Librarian of Yale University, July 1, 1905–June 30, 1906* (New Haven, CT: Tuttle, Morehouse and Taylor, 1906), 3–7; Holden, *Yale*; Carroll, *Buildings and Grounds*, 13; O'Connor, "Yale University Library," 500–505; Pinnell, *Yale University*, 33–35.

15. *Report of the Librarian, 1886–87*, quoted in O'Connor, "Yale University Library, 1865–1931," 501.

16. O'Connor, "Yale University Library," 25.

17. For Columbia College and the General Theological Seminary, see Robert A.M. Stern, Thomas Mellins, and David Fishman, *New York 1880* (New York: Monacelli, 1999), 144–54, 156–63. For Linsly Hall, see Competitive Designs, *Architectural Review* 7, no. 8 (1905), plates 50–52; Competitive Designs, *Architecture* 12, no. 2 (1905), plates 67–69; *Report of the Librarian of Yale University, July 1, 1906–June 30, 1907*, 3–7; Holden, *Yale*; Carroll, *Buildings and Grounds*, 22; O'Connor, "Yale University Library," 505–14; Pinnell, *Yale University*, 33–35.

18. Rogers letter to President Arthur Twining Hadley, quoted in Aaron Betsky, *James Gamble Rogers and the Architecture of Pragmatism* (New York: Architectural History Foundation, 1994), 247 n. 55.

19. "Where Shall Be the Library?" *Yale Alumni Weekly* 14, no. 23 (1905): 447–49.

20. For more on Low Library, see Robert A.M. Stern, Gregory Gilmartin, and John Massengale, *New York 1900* (New York: Rizzoli, 1983), 405–9; for Widener, see Matthew Battles, *Widener: Biography of a Library* (Cambridge, MA: Harvard College Library, 2004).

21. John Russell Pope, *Yale University: A Plan for Its Future Building* (New York: Cheltenham, 1919); Steven Bedford, *John Russell Pope: Architect of an Empire* (New York: Rizzoli, 1998), 160–63; Erik Vogt, "A New Yale: The Pope Plan of 1919," in Scully et al., *Yale in New Haven*, 249–61.

22. "Yale Will Build $4,000,000 Library," *New York Times,* December 15, 1923, p. 13; "Yale, 222 Years Old, Now Plans for Next Century," *New York Times,* January 27, 1924, p. XX12.

23. Pinnell, *Yale University*, 78.

24. For more on Payne Whitney Gymnasium, see Bedford, *John Russell Pope*, 165–69; Erik Vogt, "A New Yale," 253–55; Paul Goldberger, "James Gamble Rogers and the Shaping of Yale in the Twentieth Century," in Scully et al., *Yale in New Haven*, 288–89. For Calhoun College, see Bedford, *John Russell Pope*, 166–69; Goldberger, "James Gamble Rogers," 287–89.

25. Charles Harris Whitaker, ed., *Bertram Grosvenor Goodhue: Architect and Master of Many Arts* (New York: Press of the AIA, 1925), plates 111, 233–37; Richard Oliver, *Bertram Grosvenor Goodhue* (New York: Architectural History Foundation, 1983), 223–26; Betsky, *James Gamble Rogers*, 116–20; Goldberger, "James Gamble Rogers," 274–76.

26. Pinnell, *Yale University*, 81.

27. Oliver, *Bertram Grosvenor Goodhue*, 224.

28. Betsky, *James Gamble Rogers*, 119.

29. Ibid.

30. Ibid. For more on Rogers's modifications to the Pope plan to make way for Goodhue's library, see "The Yale of the Future" and "The Plan for the Physical Development of Yale University," *Yale Alumni Weekly* 33, no. 20 (1924): 523–28.

31. James J. S. Mayers quoted in Betsky, *James Gamble Rogers*, 119.

32. Oliver, *Bertram Grosvenor Goodhue*, 224.

33. See "Sterling's Lifelong Dream Comes True at Yale," *New York Times*, March 7, 1926, p. SM8; James Gamble Rogers, "Notes by the Architect," *Yale University Library Gazette* 3, no. 1 (1928): 3–7; Andrew Keogh, "Notes by the Librarian," *Yale University Library Gazette* 3, no. 1 (1928): 27–34; Ellery S. Husted, "The Sterling Memorial Library," *Yale University Library Gazette* 5, no. 4 (1931): 57–65; Lawrence A. Teasdale, "Mechanical Equipment," *Yale University Library Gazette* 5, no. 4 (1931): 66–76; William S. Snead, "The Bookstack Tower," *Yale University Library Gazette* 5, no. 4 (1931): 77–80; "The Decoration of the Sterling Memorial Library," *Yale University Library Gazette* 5, no. 4 (1931): 81–123; "Dedication of the Sterling Memorial Library," *Yale University Library Gazette* 5, no. 4 (1931): 127–55; Holden, *Yale*; Taylor, *Yale University Library*, 13–16, 23–33; Carroll, *Buildings and Grounds*, 34–35; Patricia D. Pierce, *Sparing No Detail: The Drawings of James Gamble Rogers for Yale University, 1913–1935* (New Haven, CT: Yale University Art Gallery, 1982), 18–21; Robert A.M. Stern, *Pride of Place: Building the American Dream* (New York: American Heritage, 1986), 54; Susan Ryan, "The Architecture of James Gamble Rogers at Yale University," *Perspecta* 18 (1982): 25–41; Carolyn V. Claflin, ed., *A Fitting Memorial: The Architecture and Ornament of the Sterling Memorial Library at Yale University* (New Haven, CT: Yale University Library, 2000); Schiff, "Yale University Library," in Stam, *International Dictionary of Library Histories*, 941; Michael Carey, "The Art of the Library," *Clem Labine's Traditional Building* 14, no. 2 (2001): 168–70; Goldberger, "James Gamble Rogers," 274–77.

34. See Stern, Gilmartin, and Massengale, *New York 1900*, 91–97.

35. O'Connor, "Yale University Library," 524–25.

36. Betsky, *James Gamble Rogers*, 122.

37. Rogers, "Notes by the Architect," 3–7.

38. Keogh, "Notes by the Librarian," 27–34; for the connection between the Gothic Revival and Functionalism, see, for example, Nikolaus Pevsner, *Pioneers of Modern Design: From William Morris to Walter Gropius* (London: Faber, 1936).

39. William Harlan Hale, "Art vs. Yale University," *Harkness Hoot* 1, no. 2 (1930): 17–32, quoted in "Campus Views and News," *Yale Alumni Weekly* 40, no. 9 (1930): 235–36; see also William Harlan Hale, "Yale's Cathedral Orgy," *The Nation* 132, no. 3434 (1931): 471–72; "In the Driftway," *The Nation* 132, no. 3440 (1931): 630–31; George W. Pierson, *Yale: The University College, 1921–1937* (New Haven, CT: Yale University Press, 1955), 292–94; Betsky, *James Gamble Rogers*, 58–59; Goldberger, "James Gamble Rogers," 276–77; Scully, "Modern Architecture at Yale," in Scully et al., *Yale in New Haven*, 295.

40. Hale, "Art vs. Yale University," 20–22.

41. "Art vs. Yale University," *The Arts* 17, no. 2 (1930): 125–34; "Charles Butler, F.A.I.A. Congratulates a Young Iconoclast," *American Architect* 139, no. 2591 (1931): 24–26, 126–30; "Artists vs. Yale University," *Harkness Hoot* 1, no. 3 (1931): 42–45.

42. Hale, "Yale's Cathedral Orgy," 471.

43. Hale, "Art vs. Yale University," 25.

44. William Harlan Hale, "Out of the Gargoyles and into the Future," *Horizon* 1, no. 5 (1959): 84–87.

45. Wilhelm Munthe, "A Norwegian Impression of the Building," *Yale University Library Gazette* 6 (1932): 56–58, quoted in O'Connor, "Yale University Library," 552.

46. For more on the residential college system, see Carroll L. V. Meeks, "The Yale Residential Colleges," *Yale Alumni Weekly* 43, no. 13 (1933); Carroll, *Buildings and Grounds*; Ryan, "Architecture of James Gamble Rogers," 33–39; Alex Duke, *Importing Oxbridge: English Residential Colleges and American Universities* (New Haven, CT: Yale University Press, 1996), 91–124; Goldberger, "James Gamble Rogers," 280–89.

47. Meeks, "Yale Residential Colleges"; Holden, *Yale*.

48. Meeks, "Yale Residential Colleges."

49. Carroll, *Buildings and Grounds*, 37–38.

50. Meeks, "Yale Residential Colleges"; "Calhoun College, Yale University," *Architectural Forum* 60, no. 5 (1934): 321–30.

51. Meeks, "Yale Residential Colleges."

52. Ibid.

53. See Meeks, "Yale Residential Colleges"; Paul Goldberger, Stephen Kieran, and Laurence Winnie, eds., *Berkeley: The Building of a College* (New Haven, CT: Yale University, 1999).

54. Paul Goldberger, "James Gamble Rogers and the Design of Berkeley College," in Goldberger, Kieran, and Winnie, eds., *Berkeley*, 50.

55. Peter Gisolfi, *Finding the Place of Architecture in the Landscape* (Mulgrave, Vic.: Images, 2008), 198.

56. "'Polygonal' Architecture," *Architectural Record* 127, no. 2 (1960): 159–64; "Saarinen Colleges in Situ at Yale," *Progressive Architecture* 43, no. 11 (1962): 57–60; Walter McQuade, "The New Yale Colleges," *Architectural Forum* 117 (1962): 105–11; Holden, *Yale*.

57. Frederick C. Hicks, *Yale Law School: The Founders and the Founders' Collection* (New Haven, CT: Yale University Press, 1935), 9.

58. Taylor, *Yale University Library*, 57–59.

59. Frederick C. Hicks, *Yale Law School: From the Founders to Dutton, 1845–1869*, Yale Law Library Publications 3 (New Haven, CT: Yale University Press, 1936), 25–28.

60. Frederick C. Hicks, *Yale Law School: 1869–1894, Including the County Court House Period*, Yale Law Library Publications 4 (New Haven, CT: Yale University Press, 1937), 12–15.

61. Ibid., 60. See also Montgomery Schuyler, "The Works of Cady, Berg and See," 524–31; Frederick C. Hicks, *Yale Law School: 1895–1915, Twenty Years of Hendrie Hall*, Yale Law Library Publications 7 (New Haven, CT: Yale University Press, 1938); Chamberlain, *Yale University*, 146; Lynn, "Building Yale," 160–62.

62. Taylor, *Yale University Library*, 61. For more on the Sterling Law Library, see "Yale Surveys Sites for New Buildings," *New York Times*, April 2, 1926, p. 18; "Yale Has $4,500,000 for New Law School," *New York Times*, May 20, 1927, p. 4; Yale Law Library, *Yale Law Library Manual: The Building, the Books, and Their Availability for Use*, Yale Law Library Publications 5 (New Haven, CT: Yale University Press, 1937), 1–6; Holden, *Yale*; Betsky, *James Gamble Rogers*, 127–33; Goldberger, "James Gamble Rogers," 277–78.

63. Betsky, *James Gamble Rogers*, 129.

64. Laura Kalman, *Yale Law School and the Sixties: Revolt and Reverberations* (Chapel Hill: University of North Carolina Press, 2005), 210–13.

65. Charles K. Hoyt, "The Yale Law School Library and Lecture Hall," *Architectural Record* 166, no. 1 (1979): 111–14; *Herbert S. Newman and Partners* (Mulgrave, Vic.: Images, 1999), 80–81.

66. Carey, "The Art of the Library"; David Dillon, *The Architecture of Kallmann McKinnell and Wood* (New York: Edizioni, 2004), 143; Kallmann McKinnell and Wood Architects, "Law School Renovation, Sterling Law Buildings, Yale University," unpublished project description.

67. Phil Fortino, "Yale U.'s Renovated Law Library Will Recapture Sociability," *Yale Daily News*, February 24, 1999.

68. "Yale Plans Start on Divinity 'Quad,'" *New York Times*, May 4, 1931, p. 5; "The Yale Divinity School, New Haven, Conn.," *Architecture* 67 (1933): 269–75; William Adams Delano, "The Reminiscences of William Adams Delano," William Adams Delano Papers, Yale University Manuscripts and Archives, 1950; Holden, *Yale*; Pinnell, *Yale University*, 160–62; Peter Pennoyer and Anne Walker, *The Architecture of Delano and Aldrich* (New York: W. W. Norton, 2003), 170–73; Lynn, "Building Yale," 224–27.

69. Aldrich, "Reminiscences," 54–55.

70. Christopher Wigren, "The Yale Divinity School: Another View," *Connecticut Preservation News* 27, no. 1 (2004): 9; *R. M. Kliment and Frances Halsband Architects* (Mulgrave, Vic.: Images, 2008), 45–57.

71. William Adams Delano, "Sage Hall," *Yale Alumni Weekly* 31, no. 23 (1922): 558–59; "The Dedication of Sage Hall," *Yale Alumni Weekly* 33, no. 25 (1924): 683–86; Taylor, *Yale University Library*, 56–57; Carroll, *Buildings and Grounds*, 30.

72. "Library for the History of Medicine at Yale University," *Science* 90, no. 2339 (1939): 389; "Nearly Completed Medical Library to House Outstanding Collections," *Yale Daily News*, January 28, 1941, p. 2; "The Dedication of the Yale Medical Library," *Science* 93, no. 2423 (1941): 535; "The Yale Medical Library," *Pencil Points* 23, no. 1 (1942): 31–36; John F. Fulton, *Harvey Cushing: A Biography* (Springfield, IL:

Charles C. Thomas, 1946), 646–49, 663–67, 711–13; *The Making of a Library: Extracts from Letters 1934–1941 of Harvey Cushing, Arnold C. Klebs, John F. Fulton* (New Haven, CT: Yale University, 1959); Holden, *Yale*; Taylor, *Yale University Library*, 62–67; Patrick J. O'Connor, "A Time of Choice," *Yale Medicine* 16, no. 1 (1981): 2–6; Pinnell, *Yale University*, 171–72; Toby A. Appel, "A 'Trinatarian Plan': The Historical Library, Cushing/Whitney Medical Library, Yale University," *Watermark* 25, no. 4 (2002): 65–69; Toby A. Appel with Ned Pocengal, "The Medical Library at Yale, 1701–2001," Yale School of Medicine, http://www.med.yale.edu/library/exhibits/medicallibrary/; Peter Pennoyer and Anne Walker, *The Architecture of Grosvenor Atterbury* (New York: W. W. Norton, 2009), 249–51.

73. Klebs to Cushing in *The Making of a Library*, 50.

74. Alexander Purves and Allan J. Dehar, "The Design of the Harvey Cushing/John Hay Whitney Medical Library," in the Harvey Cushing/John Hay Whitney Medical Library Dedication Program (New Haven, CT: Yale University School of Medicine, 1990); "Interiors Showcase," *American Libraries* 22, no. 4 (1991): 344–53; Linda M. Wilkins, "Materials Make the Difference," *Connecticut Architect and Specifier* 4, no. 3 (1991): 37–39.

75. Nicholas Adams, *Skidmore, Owings and Merrill: SOM Since 1936* (Milan: Electa, 2006), 184; see also "SOM Designs Onyx Shelter for Yale's Rare Books," *Architectural Record* 128, no. 5 (1960): 44; "Rare Building for Rare Books," *Architectural Forum* 113, no. 5 (1960): 139–41; "Rare Book and Manuscript Library, Yale University," *Architectural Design* 31, no. 2 (1961): 85; "Yale's New Vault: Material/Structural Analysis," *Progressive Architecture* 42 (1961): 152–59; Harry Gilroy, "Yale to Dedicate Library Building," *New York Times*, October 11, 1963, p. 33; "Rare Book Library at Yale Dedicated," *Architectural Record* 134, no. 5 (1963): 12–13; "Yale Rare Book and Manuscript Library," *Progressive Architecture* 45, no. 2 (1964): 130–33; Skidmore, Owings and Merrill, "The Beinecke Rare Book and Manuscript Library," *Yale University Library Gazette* 38, no. 4 (1964): 127–30; Vincent Scully, "Architecture and Man at Yale," *Saturday Review*, May 23, 1964, pp. 26–29; "Bibliothèque à l'Université de Yale," *l'Architecture d'Aujourd'hui* 34, no. 117 (November 1964–January 1965): 62–67; Ellsworth Mason, "The Beinecke Siamese Twins," *College and Research Libraries* 26, no. 3 (1965): 199–212; "Rare Book Library," *Architecture International* 1 (1965): 88–95; Holden, *Yale*; Hobson, *Great Libraries*, 232; Taylor, *Yale University Library*, 36–42; Carroll, *Buildings and Grounds*, 10–11; Carol Herselle Krinsky, *Gordon Bunshaft of Skidmore, Owings and Merrill* (New York: Architectural History Foundation, 1988), 141–46, 190–99; Pinnell, *Yale University*, 113–14; "Beinecke Rare Book and Manuscript Library," *A+U Extra Edition* (November 2003): 162–65; Patrick L. Pinnell, "Beinecke at Forty: Still Truth into Light," in Stephen Parks, ed., *The Beinecke Library of Yale University* (New Haven, CT: Beinecke Library, 2003), 26–51; Scully, "Modern Architecture at Yale," 320–22.

76. Scully, "Architecture and Man at Yale," 28.

77. See Phyllis Lambert, ed., *Mies in America* (New York: Whitney Museum of American Art, 2001), 462–74.

78. Scully, "Modern Architecture at Yale," 320–21.

79. "Yale's New Art and Architecture Building," *Architectural Record* 131, no. 1 (1962): 16; Jonathan Barnett, "A School for the Arts at Yale," *Architectural Record* 135, no. 2 (1964): 111–20; Paul Rudolph, "Yale Art and Architecture Building," *Arts and Architecture* 81, no. 2 (1964): 26–35; Walter McQuade, "Yale School of Art and Architecture: The Building," *Architectural Forum* 120, no. 2 (1964): 66–74; Sibyl Moholy-Nagy, "Yale's School of Art and Architecture: The Measure," *Architectural Forum* 120, no. 2 (1964): 76–79; Paul Rudolph, "Yale Art and Architecture Building," *Architectural Design* 34 (1964): 161, 178–80; Vincent Scully, "Art and Architecture Building, Yale University," *Architectural Review* 135, no. 807 (1964): 324–32; Sibyl Moholy-Nagy and Gerhard Schwab, *The Architecture of Paul Rudolph* (New York: Praeger, 1970), 120–33; Richard Pommer, "The Art and Architecture Building at Yale, Once Again," *Burlington Magazine* 114, no. 837 (1972): 853–61; Taylor, *Yale University Library*, 53; Carroll, *Buildings and Grounds*, 7–8; Jules Prown, "On Being a Client," *Journal of the Society of Architectural Historians* 42, no. 1 (1983): 11–14.

80. McQuade, "Yale School of Art and Architecture," 69.

81. Scully, "Art and Architecture Building," 325.

82. Prown, "On Being a Client," 12.

83. Quoted from John W. Cook and Heinrich Klotz, *Conversations with Architects* (New York: Praeger, 1973), 99.

84. For more on the renovation, see Hannah Bennett, "The Robert B. Haas Family Arts Library Opening," *Nota Bene* 23, no. 2 (2008): 1.

85. Vincent Scully, "The Case for Preservation," *Yale Daily News,* April 11, 1967, p. 2; "No Iron Ball," *Yale Daily News,* April 11, 1967, p. 2; "Yale's 'Ugliest' Get Set for Demolition," *Yale Daily News,* April 27, 1967, p. 1; "New Engineering Center Opens Doors Tomorrow," *Yale Daily News,* February 20, 1970, p. 1; Vincent Scully, "Becton Belongs in Goo-Goo Land," *Yale Daily News,* February 26, 1970, p. 3; Tician Papachristou, *Marcel Breuer: New Buildings and Projects* (New York: Praeger, 1970), 161–63; Don Metz, *New Architecture in New Haven*, rev. ed. (Cambridge, MA: MIT Press, 1973), 44–45; Taylor, *Yale University Library,* 56; Carroll, *Buildings and Grounds,* 10; Isabelle Hyman, *Marcel Breuer, Architect: The Career and the Buildings* (New York: Harry N. Abrams, 2001), 202.

86. "Recent Work of Philip Johnson," *Architectural Record* 132, no. 1 (1962): 113–15; "Kline Science Center, Yale University," *Architectural Record* 135, no. 4 (1964): 148–49; James T. Burns, "Locus for Gown, Focus for Town," *Progressive Architecture* 48, no. 2 (1967): 90–97; "The Kline Tower at Yale," *Architectural Record* 141, no. 7 (1967): 140–45; John A. Harrison, "The Kline Science Center Library," *Yale University Library Gazette* 42, no. 3 (1968): 154–57; Charles Noble and Yukio Futagawa, *Philip Johnson* (London: Thames and Hudson, 1972); Brown, *New Haven,* 144; Taylor, *Yale University Library,* 45–48; Pinnell, *Yale University,* 164–65.

87. Taylor, *Yale University Library,* 16–17, 48–52; Carroll, *Buildings and Grounds,* 35; *Edward Larrabee Barnes, Architect* (New York: Rizzoli, 1994), 243; Pinnell, *Yale University,* 92–93.

88. "Library Plans Expansion," *Yale Daily News,* March 7, 1967, p. 1; Bob Mascia, "Students Save X-Campus," *Yale Daily News,* Summer 1968, p. 8; Hunter Morrison and Hugh Spitzer, "Maze of Committees Keeps Dissent Quiet," *Yale Daily News,* Summer 1968, p. 12; Tom Linden, "Activism and the SDS," *Yale Daily News,* Summer 1968, pp. 14–15; "New Plans Feature Moats for Underground Library," *Yale Daily News,* September 16, 1968, p. 3; John Coots, "Barnes to Discuss Plans," *Yale Daily News,* November 25, 1968, p. 1; "Campus Planning," *Yale Daily News,* November 25, 1968, p. 2; John Coots, "Architect to Discuss Sterling Library Plans," *Yale Daily News,* December 2, 1968, p. 1; "Library Program Altered; Architect Airs Designs," *Yale Daily News,* December 3, 1968, p. 1; Manfred Ibel, Walter Langsam, and Herb Short, "Three Views on Library Designs," *Yale Daily News,* December 10, 1968, pp. 4–6; Tom Anderson, "Blum Reveals Library Plan; Students Indicate Approval," *Yale Daily News,* March 13, 1969, pp. 1, 6; "John Blum Expounds Cross Campus Plans," *Yale Daily News,* April 8, 1969, p. 3; Rose Ananthanayagam, "CCL Airport in Eighth Year," *Yale Daily News,* March 27, 1979, p. 3; Scully, "Modern Architecture at Yale," 336.

89. Pinnell, *Yale University,* 93.

90. See Jeff Muskus, "CCL Progresses to Design Phase of Renovations," *Yale Daily News,* October 19, 2004; Jeff Muskus, "Builders Reveal Plans for CCL," *Yale Daily News,* March 25, 2005; Cullen Macbeth, "Architects Discuss Furniture for CCL," *Yale Daily News,* November 16, 2006; Tyler Hill, "Book Lover Gives Big to CCL," *Yale Daily News,* December 1, 2006; Noah Lawrence, "Real Beauty of Bass Extends Beyond Its Luxury," *Yale Daily News,* October 22, 2007; Yonah Freemark, "Wood-Varnished Bass Improves on CCL . . . Sort of," *Yale Daily News,* November 30, 2007; Robert Daigle, "The Bass Library Grand Opening," *Nota Bene* 22, no. 2 (Fall 2007): 1–2; Mark Alden Branch, "*This* Is CCL?" *Yale Alumni Magazine*, January/February 2008.

91. Quoted in Branch, "*This* Is CCL?"

92. Brooks Shepard, Jr., "Yale's Music Library Revised," *Notes* 13, no. 3 (1956): 421–23; Taylor, *Yale University Library,* 67–68; Juanita Dugdale, "Rhapsody in Blue," *Interiors* 158, no. 8 (1999): 60–63.

93. Jules David Prown, *The Architecture of the Yale Center for British Art* (New Haven, CT: Yale University, 1977); "The Yale Center for British Art," *Burlington Magazine* 119, no. 890 (1977): 315; Vincent Scully, "Yale Center for British Art," *Architectural Record* 161, no. 7 (1977): 95–104; William Jordy, "Kahn at Yale," *Architectural Review* 162, no. 965 (1977): 37–44; Andrea O. Dean, "A Legacy of Light," *AIA Journal* 67, no. 6 (1978): 82–89; Carroll, *Buildings and Grounds,* 8–10; Michael J. Crosbie, "Evaluation: Monument Before Its Time," *Architecture* 75, no. 1 (1986): 64–67; Patricia Cummings Loud, *The Art Museums of Louis I. Kahn* (Durham, NC: Duke University Press, 1989), 173–243, especially 179, 195, 220; Duncan Robinson, *The Yale Center for British Art: A Tribute to the Genius of Louis I. Kahn* (New Haven, CT: Yale University Press, 1997).

94. Prown, *Architecture of the Yale Center for British Art,* 17.

95. Robinson, *Yale Center for British Art,* 48.

96. Scully, "Yale Center for British Art," 103.

97. "A Sensitive Storehouse for Burgeoning Knowledge," *Architectural Record* 171, no. 9 (1983): 86–90; Scully, "Modern Architecture at Yale," 337. See also Pinnell, *Yale University*, 151–52.

98. "Life Explores World's Finest Walpole Library," *Life,* October 23, 1944, pp. 116–21; see also John Cornforth, "The Cowles-Lewis House, Farmington—I," *Country Life,* April 27, 1978, pp. 1150–53; John Cornforth, "The Cowles-Lewis House, Farmington—II," *Country Life,* May 4, 1978, pp. 1230–33; LuAnn Bishop, "The Lewis Walpole Library: A Piece of Yale in Farmington," *Yale Bulletin and Calendar,* June 24–July 22, 1996; Ross Goldberg, "University Presents Library Plans," *Yale Daily News,* April 7, 2006; Ross Goldberg, "Commission Approves Renovation Plans to Library After Month-Long Deadlock," *Yale Daily News,* April 11, 2006; Amanda Patrick and Maggie Powell, "The Lewis Walpole Library Reopens," *Nota Bene* 22, no. 2 (Fall 2007): 3; Mark Alden Branch, "Yale's Country House Gets a Makeover," *Yale Alumni Magazine,* January/February 2008; Lewis Walpole Library Board of Managers, "The Renovation of the Library," the Lewis Walpole Library, http://library.yale.edu/walpole/html/information/renovation.html.

99. Cornforth, "The Cowles-Lewis House, Farmington—II"; see also Pennoyer and Walker, *Architecture of Delano and Aldrich*, 192.

100. Centerbrook Architects and Planners, "Lewis Walpole Library, Yale University," http://www.centerbrook.com/Project%20Profiles/YaleWalpole.htm.

101. Gilbert McCoy Troxell, "The Elizabethan Club: Its Origins and Its Books," *Yale University Library Gazette* 27, no. 1 (1952): 19–28; Holden, *Yale*; Carroll, *Buildings and Grounds*, 17; Stephen Parks, *The Elizabethan Club of Yale University and Its Library* (New Haven, CT: Yale University Press, 1986); Pinnell, *Yale University*, 90.

102. Kenneth Boroson Architects, unpublished project description, 2009.

103. "Day Missions Library, Yale University," *Brickbuilder* 22, no. 11 (1913): plates 167–68; Pennoyer and Walker, *Architecture of Delano and Aldrich*, 185; Lynn, "Building Yale," 124–25.

104. Carroll, *Buildings and Grounds*, 88; Lynn, "Building Yale," 123–24.

A group photograph taken in September 1962 at the topping-off ceremony for the Beinecke Library. From left to right: J. Gordon Kenefick, Thomas E. Marston, Edwin J. Beinecke, James T. Babb, Frederick W. Beinecke, Howard B. Gotlieb, David Roy Watkins, Vera Barry, Marjorie G. Wynne, Robert J. Olson, F. Bernice Field, Donald C. Gallup, Archibald Hanna, Jr., Dale R. Roylance, and Donald G. Wing.
Beinecke Rare Book and Manuscript Library, Yale University, Photographs (RU 106).
Manuscripts and Archives, Yale University Library.

MARJORIE G. WYNNE

Crossing Wall

Marjorie Wynne died at her home in Hamden, Connecticut, on April 5, 2009. Miss Wynne, as she was known to rare book and special collections librarians around the world, and to generations of students and faculty at Yale, joined the Yale University Library in 1942 and retired in 1987. This essay originally appeared in The Beinecke Library of Yale University, *published in 2003. It is reprinted here as a tribute to a spirited, wise, and generous colleague.*

The Sterling Memorial Library was twelve years old when I walked through its massive doors on a September morning in 1942. Everything was new and wonderful: the towering nave swept boldly forward (unhindered by a central staircase), and every surface—glass, iron, stone, and wood—was alive with scenes and inscriptions from books and manuscripts.

The Rare Book Room, where I worked with Chauncey Tinker and, later, Herman Liebert, was the most elegant space in the new building, but unfortunately it was not air conditioned and eventually not big enough. By the late fifties the shelves that had been half-empty when I arrived were full to overflowing, and certain modern literary collections had, of necessity, been transferred to a locked area in the main library stacks.

It was at this critical moment—and with the skillful guidance of James T. Babb, the University Librarian—that three Beinecke brothers and their families decided to give Yale a new building just for rare books and manuscripts. This was a blissful prospect for me and for the curators of three other collections in Sterling, for it meant that one day we would be able to move into a new building with space galore and a climate suitable for books and people. It was also, of course, the end of our separate little empires.

The architect for the new building was Gordon Bunshaft of Skidmore, Owings and Merrill. I never met Mr. Bunshaft, nor, I think, did the other curators, but from time to time Mr. Babb would bring us word of an emerging and imaginative design combining marble walls, an interior glass tower, a sunken courtyard, and miles of underground shelving. On February 15, 1960, a large model of the new building was unveiled in the nave of the Sterling Library, and we were thoroughly dazzled by this gleaming object that promised, when made real, to change our daily lives.

Ground was broken in Hewitt Quadrangle on May 1, 1961, the deafening evacuation was finally finished, and a building began to grow inside a huge protective covering. On *our* side of Wall Street we had much to do in preparation for the move now scheduled for August 1963: catalogues of the four separate collections had to be interfiled and new subject cards added; a large new reference collection had to be created and catalogued; hundreds of rare books in the Sterling stacks had to be identified and prepared for transfer; the Rare Book Room manuscript catalogue, on five-by-eight cards, had to be retyped on standard three-by-five cards; routines and procedures had to be established; a sensible shelving plan had to be designed; and two large cases and twenty-two small exhibition cases had to be filled before the opening ceremony.

This was a time of intense activity and, at least for me, of intense emotion. For twenty years I had cherished every feature of the Rare Book Room — the rich paneling, the painted ceiling, the carved Jacobean screen, the leaded glass doors on the bookcases, the quotation at the top of the monumental iron gates: "There is no past so long as books shall live."

As I prepared to leave this setting so full of special memories, I was further saddened by the death of Mr. Tinker on March 17, 1963. For the past eight years he had lived comfortably in Wethersfield, near his sister, but he had forgotten the Rare Book Room, and he had forgotten me. He knew nothing of the marble building now free of its cocoon, but *we* knew that in a very special way he was its true progenitor. Years ago he had exhorted Yale to acquire ever more research materials if it hoped to claim a superior position among university libraries, and he had then done more than anyone else to secure that position by his activities as Keeper of Rare Books, by the gift of his illustrious private collection, and most especially by his extraordinary influence on generations of students — the Beinecke brothers, Frank Altschul, Wilmarth Lewis, Paul Mellon among them — who would in time become brilliant collectors and generous donors.

At five o'clock on the last day of June 1963 we locked the doors of the Rare Book Room forever. Mr. Liebert, recently appointed Librarian of the Beinecke Rare Book and Manuscript Library, opened a bottle of sherry, we drank a few toasts, and I made my way home in a cloak of melancholy. Early the next morning, back in the Rare Book Room in a very different set of work clothes, I met the crew from Cohen & Powell and for the next six weeks supervised the packing of books and manuscripts — all day, every day.

The actual move began on August 12, and Kenneth Nesheim, the new assistant librarian of Beinecke, arrived just in time to oversee that operation. The boxes were moved from the Rare Book Room to the Cohen & Powell vans at the Wall Street door, driven around the block, and delivered to the front entrance of Beinecke.

The first books to be shelved were English literature, starting on the perimeter of the second level of the glass tower and continuing to the sixth and highest level. Every shelf, by design, was left partly empty to allow for expansion, and the shelves inside the tower (invisible to the public) were left completely empty. The shelves at ground level were reserved for incunabula, then numbering about three thousand. Here, the oldest books in the library were just a few feet from visitors who have always been fascinated by the bindings — some original, others very early, some with labels, one or two dangling part of a chain.

The rest of the material from the Rare Book Room was shelved in the underground stacks, and so too were the Collection of American Literature

Watercolor by George Rudolph of the interior of the Beinecke Rare Book and Manuscript Library, 1963. *Architectural Drawings and Maps of Yale University Building and Grounds (RU 1). Manuscripts and Archives.*

(Donald Gallup, curator) and the Collection of Western Americana (Archibald Hanna, Jr., curator). At this point, all moving was temporarily suspended. It was August 28, and we had thirty-one working days to prepare for the dedication ceremony on October 11.

With the glass tower full of books, the marble walls aflame on sunny days, the two curved cases at the top of the stairs leading up to the mezzanine filled with selections from Edwin J. Beinecke's Robert Louis Stevenson collection on the south side and Frederick W. Beinecke's collection of Western Americana on the north; with dark leather chairs and olive burl tables on the mezzanine and bronze exhibition cases on both levels, this monumental space began to look warm, luxurious, and inviting.

The scene below ground was altogether different. This was the level where the reading room and offices wrapped around a white marble courtyard. The card catalogues were here, also the service desk, work space, and staff lounge. By mid-October this would be the heart of the library, but at the moment, with its expanse of stark white walls and light beige carpet, it looked singularly cold and antiseptic.

But not for long. Lots of paintings were being hung: in the lobby, a wonderfully dark and haunting portrait of Alice Toklas by Dora Maar next to Picabia's monolithic Gertrude Stein, and in the reading room, portraits of Mr. Tinker, Mr. Lewis, and Mr. Babb. Curators were choosing favorite things to hang in their offices and nearby corridors.

The lobby began to look more colorful and attractive, and its appearance was further improved by the arrival of several huge potted plants ordered by the architect. Mr. Liebert hated them on sight, fussed and fumed, and then threatened to poison them. While two workmen stood by, uncertain of what to do next, I motioned to them to pick up a large ficus, to follow me down the hall and into my office, and there to put it in a bright corner. Other plants were put in the staff lounge and in the lobby, where they all withered after a few years, but not because they were poisoned. Mr. Liebert, I think, would not have defied the architect, even if Donald Gallup had not already been ordered to put the furniture he had rearranged in his office exactly where the architect had left it until after the key to the library had been presented to the University.

And so it was presented on the afternoon of Friday, October 11, by Edwin J. Beinecke to Wilmarth Lewis (on behalf of the Corporation) and then to Mr. Liebert. The invited audience for this ceremony was relatively small, almost a family affair. Chairs were arranged around the reception desk on the ground level, some of us sat on the mezzanine steps, and Mr. Lewis made a short speech. Mr. Beinecke was given a gold copy of the library key embedded in Lucite, and three gifts from the library staff were arranged in a nearby exhibition case: a Stevenson letter in honor of Edwin J. Beinecke, a letter from a California forty-niner in honor of Frederick W. Beinecke, and a rare first printing of Edmond Hoyle's *Short Treatise on the Game of Whist* in memory of the late Walter Beinecke. After the ceremony, members of the Corporation withdrew to Woodbridge Hall and in the course of the evening elected Kingman Brewster, Jr., as the next President of the University, succeeding Whitney Griswold, who had died on April 19.

On Saturday there was a reception for the people who had built the library, and several weeks later a large open house for the citizens of New Haven.

On Monday, October 14, the library was opened to the public, and scholars and visitors arrived in numbers. In late November, the fourth major collection in Sterling, German Literature, was moved into Beinecke with its curator Curt von Faber du Faur. Various smaller collections came later—for example, the books known to have been at Yale when the first catalogue was published in 1743 (now on shelves near the incunabula in the glass tower), and one new collection—mainly eighteenth-century books and manuscripts—was established through the gift of James Marshall and Marie-Louise Osborn.

So began life in an architectural monument unlike any I had ever seen before. Was everything perfect? Of course not. There was no closet in my office for coats or anything else (a hook eventually appeared on the back of the door); the white plaster kept falling off the walls on the court level; and to this day the dysfunctional locks on the two long exhibition cases occasionally bite off keys and constantly frustrate everybody who installs an exhibition. But scholars loved the light in the reading room, visitors were stunned by the glass tower filled with books, and donors came bearing gifts.

I missed the beauty of the building materials in Sterling, the wit and playfulness of its decoration, but inevitably I began to grow accustomed to the cool, clean look of the court level at Beinecke and especially to the comforts of my office. It was *large*, and my desk was large, and behind my desk there was a long credenza with a wall of bookshelves above and a row of black filing drawers below. Marie Laurenein's lovely pink and gray portrait of a poodle (Gertrude Stein's Basket) hung on the wall to my left, and in the corridor outside were portraits of Barrie, Conrad, and Stevenson. The wall to my right, facing south, was all glass, and when the vertical blinds were open I could see only the white marble courtyard and the offices around it, a small patch of ever-changing sky, and the tips of a few tall trees near Berkeley College.

The courtyard is the garden of the library, said Isamu Noguchi, who designed it, and in the garden he put three smooth white marble sculptures. The pyramid, he said, represents the geometry of the earth, the apex of which introduces another point of infinity. The large circular disc is the sun, the coiled magnet, a ring of energy, and the cube, standing on one point, signifies chance.

The pyramid was just outside my window, and thus for the next twenty-four years I lived and worked behind a point of infinity. The ficus that I had so shamelessly kidnapped had an honored place by the window, where it too remained for twenty-four years, with an occasional refreshing visit to the greenhouse and a bit of surgery now and then by Frederick Pottle, one of its admirers.

In 1924 when Mr. Tinker spoke to an assembly of alumni about plans to build the Sterling Memorial Library, he said that he looked forward to having "not merely a fine house for bookish people to live in, but a great treasury of books to put in it as its soul and its center."

In crossing Wall, I and all the curators moved from a fine Gothic house to a fine modern one where we continued to collect, preserve, and make available the treasury that is its soul and center.

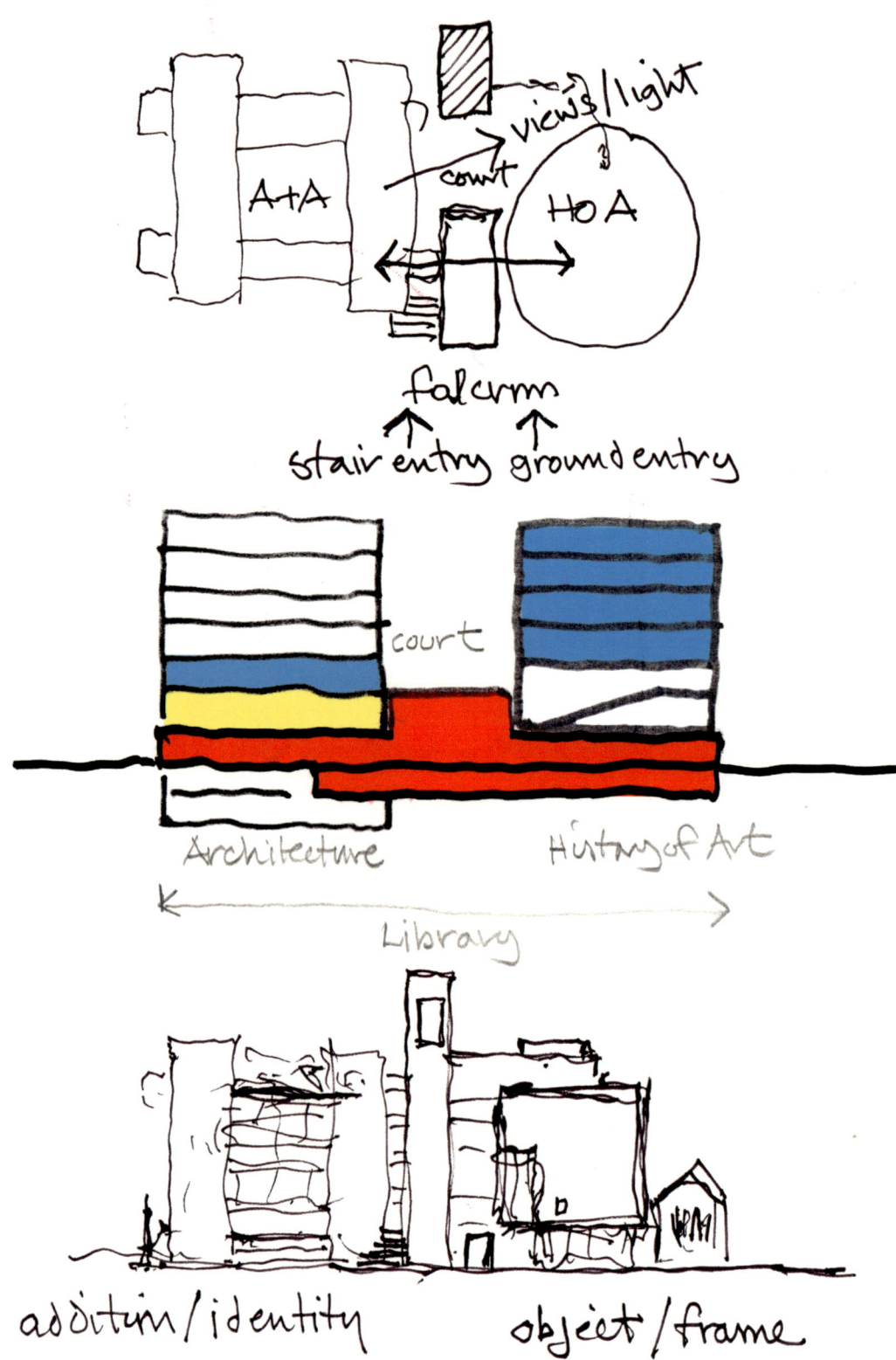

Charles Gwathmey's conceptual designs for the renovated Art + Architecture Building and new building for the History of Art Department.
Gwathmey Siegel and Associates.

CHARLES GWATHMEY

Reconstituting the Legacy

Charles Gwathmey died in New York on August 3, 2009, two months after he completed this essay describing his bold and engaging vision for Rudolph Hall, Loria Center, and Haas Family Arts Library. A graduate of the Yale School of Architecture, he founded Gwathmey Siegel and Associates with Robert Siegel in 1968. His architectural legacy includes the renovated Rudolph Hall, the addition to the Guggenheim Museum in New York, the Museum of the Moving Image in Astoria, Queens, the renovated Whig Hall at Princeton, the International Center of Photography in New York, and a number of private residences around the world.

To have been selected as the architect to renovate and restore Paul Rudolph's Art + Architecture Building and design an addition for the History of Art Department was a unique and challenging opportunity.

Resurrecting a modern masterwork, which had been physically and critically maligned, disrespected, and unmaintained from its initial dedication in 1963, as well as reconfirming Paul Rudolph's contributions as both a major modern visionary architect and great teacher, were a personal commitment and obligation for me. He was a mentor and lifelong friend whom I admired and respected both professionally and personally.

Fittingly, the renovated Art + Architecture Building was renamed Paul Rudolph Hall by the major benefactor, Sid Bass. The addition was named the Jeffrey H. Loria Center for the History of Art, while the library, combining the Art + Architecture and Drama Libraries, as well as the Arts of the Book Collection and the Visual Resources Collection, became the Robert B. Haas Family Arts Library.

The original Art + Architecture Library was consolidated on the ground level of Rudolph's building. The entry was obscured and without street presence or identity, and the library had long outgrown its space. A major requirement from library staff was that the entry be visible and accessible from the street and new lobby. They also requested that the redesigned space be contiguous and more than double in area to accommodate an expanded new information and reference desk with adjacent support offices for an increased staff; a teaching classroom; three study rooms; secured and monitored special collections spaces including offices, compact shelving, a reading room, and classroom; exhibition display cases for rare books and artifacts; general reference compact shelving; new reference shelving; a restored periodical room and study carrel mezzanine with interpretive replication of Rudolph's reading tables to accommodate twenty-first-century technology, banquettes, shelves, and built-in benches; and, finally, a restored courtyard on Chapel Street that would emit natural light on the south side of the reading room.

Charles Gwathmey, 1938–2009. *William Taufic.*

The architectural and philosophical design strategy was to render the library as the programmatic and physical bridge that would connect Rudolph Hall and the Loria Center and act as the common intellectual domain where students from the various disciplines would share and engage. The new "Great Hall," a three-story, skylit volume, was designed to be the central passageway and multi-use referential/orientation space connecting the two buildings.

Researchers and students now enter the Haas Family Arts Library from the new ground floor Loria Center lobby, which is visible from the restored ceremonial stair on York Street and the second-level Rudolph Hall entry lobby, affording the library increased visibility and presence. The third-floor skylit roof of the Great Hall, transformed as an iconic, memorable facade both inside and out, is viewed from the fourth through seventh floors of both the Architecture and History of Art buildings. It is rendered as the reinterpretation of Rudolph's courtyard between the original structure and the former Gentree Men's Store, which was adjacent to the Yale Daily News building. The entire project is architecturally and environmentally interlocked, conceived as a collage composition. The Loria Center is intended to be both deferential to Rudolph Hall while simultaneously establishing its own architectural presence as a contextual bridge to the Yale Daily News building and Yale's historic campus to the north.

Paul Rudolph's Art + Architecture Building, 1963. *Ezra Stoller © Esto.*

Exterior view of Rudolph Hall and Loria Center from York Street, 2008. *Peter Aaron © Esto.*

Special collections reading room and circulating collection stacks.
Peter Aaron © Esto.

Left. View of the Robert B. Haas Family Arts Library from Rudolph Hall's entry lobby. *Peter Aaron © Esto.*

Above. Views of the restored periodical and study space. *Michael Marsland, Yale University.*

Green roof and view of Rudolph Hall from the Loria Center.
Peter Aaron © Esto.

Frontispiece. The New Library with a view into the Long Hall. *Peter Aaron © Esto.*

MARK SIMON

The Lewis Walpole Library Puzzle

STARTING OUT

It was exciting to learn that Centerbrook Architects and Planners had been selected to design renovations and additions to Yale's Lewis Walpole Library in Farmington, Connecticut. The library is an internationally recognized research institute for eighteenth-century studies and the primary center for the study of Horace Walpole (1717–97) and his house, Strawberry Hill. The library's collection of Walpoliana includes half of the traceable volumes from Walpole's Strawberry Hill library and many of his letters and manuscripts. Its collections also include significant holdings of other eighteenth-century British books, manuscripts, prints, drawings, and paintings, as well as important examples of the era's decorative arts. The library runs an active fellowship program and sponsors conferences, lectures, and exhibitions in cooperation with other Yale libraries and departments.

Annie Burr Lewis and her husband, Wilmarth Sheldon "Lefty" Lewis, Class of 1918, a preeminent scholar of Walpole, gave their collection along with their eighteenth-century Farmington property to Yale University in 1980. The entire farmstead included the Cowles House (the Lewises' eighteenth-century house), a 1920s "New Library" addition by architects Delano and Aldrich, a mid-twentieth-century garage and squash court additions, the adjacent eighteenth-century Timothy Root House used to house visiting researchers, a two-hundred-and-fifty-year-old building lodging a museum of Indian artifacts, and a barn that functioned as a workshop. The original house and its twentieth-century additions were, however, ill suited to the needs of an important research institution and lacked suitable meeting and study spaces, collections and archival storage, modern conservation facilities, climate control, and modern security. Little did we know what an interesting conundrum awaited when we took this project on.

UNCOVERING THE PUZZLE

We began our work with an effort to understand the place and the people of "the Walpole." After initial discussions with the Librarian, Margaret K. Powell, the Yale Facilities team, and the Walpole's Board of Managers, we suggested interactive workshops to gather and share ideas and opinions from all involved. We find that this approach helps clients and architects march together. It also allows the architects to learn more than just the facts and figures of an institution, as the sessions reveal a place's character and culture. As rarely happens in normal planning interviews, our client team members are able to hear their compatriots' views and discover that their individual needs and preferences differ. They also learn about the upcoming trials of schedules, budgets, and priorities.

In 2003 we gathered representatives from the Board of Managers, staff,

Figure 1. Centerbrook and library staff, students, and members of the community walk the Lewis Walpole Library site during renovation project planning. *Centerbrook Architects and Planners, LLP.*

Yale librarians, students, scholars, and several library neighbors to walk the site together and to discuss key elements, views, and existing conditions [fig. 1]. We also held extensive interviews with the library staff. Those exercises prompted the daunting realization that while the group members agreed on four important priorities for the project, those priorities were not compatible. Their four priorities were to protect the library's extraordinary collections; make those accessible to staff, scholars, and, to a degree, the public; protect and preserve the eighteenth-century Cowles House and its important additions; and make the house itself more accessible to staff, scholars, and visiting researchers.

It was clear at the time that the library's collections were at risk from inadequate climate control and susceptible to fire and flood. Researchers were spread between two small rooms, requiring the staffing of two reading rooms, and collections were housed in cramped storage spaces. There was no dedicated classroom or lecture space, and exhibitions were restricted to a narrow hallway. Staff desks were everywhere, including in the garage, in former maids' rooms in the Lewis house, and in a passageway between the stacks and a lavatory. Materials conservation and restoration work was being done in a small upstairs bedroom. The old house was not secure, and interior circulation patterns made visitor control difficult. We also realized that it would be almost impossible to upgrade the old house to modern standards for collections care and storage without tearing it down and rebuilding it. At the same time, any attempt at modernization and expansion needed to respect the library's setting and its status as a historic site along a historic street in a historic village. An addition would have to connect to the original house to be functionally integrated, yet it appeared that the required new space would dwarf the original.

The grounds of the Lewis Walpole site also demanded respect. Several courtyard gardens behind the house were designed by Annie Burr Lewis. The house looks west over these gardens and an extensive lawn toward the rest of the fourteen-acre property with its notable specimen trees and landscape venues, as well as tilled farm fields, forest, and wetlands adjacent to the Pequabuck River just south of its junction with the Farmington River.

Centerbrook and Yale also wanted to make the project sustainable. In 2003 Yale had just launched its drive to become a leader in environmental stewardship. For our part, Centerbrook had been pioneers in this direction for thirty years, so we were delighted to see new interest in sustainable design practices. This meant using minimal energy, providing a healthy indoor environment, recycling materials during and after construction, maximizing daylight (without possible harm to library collections), and finding renewable sources for heating and cooling. The site also required using native species in planting, working with the local climate, and absorbing storm water from driveway and parking areas.

LOOKING FOR OPTIONS

We thought that a modern-style addition would cause the delicately framed and ornamented original to suffer. Many contemporary architects have added glass-clad additions to historic structures, believing that glass would all but disappear. Visits to a few of these had convinced us that this strategy would not work here since the addition would be highly visible in the middle of the property. In other locations, those geometric objects might fade away as connections between strong old buildings or as delicate additions tucked off to the side. Here, though, anything strikingly different would become the center of attention and would slight the houses surrounding it. The Cowles House is also close to the roads on two sides, and we could not build on to the New Library addition on the back without ruining it. Simply put, there was no place to hide the addition. The Cowles House is delicate and domestically scaled, the essence of eighteenth-century New England, and a large house-like appendage would be odd. Many an old small inn has been ruined with later mimetic additions that threw off or overwhelmed the balance of the original; we did not want the addition to seem swollen or obese.

We have found that the best architecture has a wholeness to it, an integrity where the parts feel as if they belong. Adding a house to a house can create a freak, a two-headed monster. How could this domicile accommodate an institution? How could we let the Cowles House (and the Root House for that matter) maintain their individual identities while accommodating collections and a community of scholars?

The answer lay in a barn. Barns, as any tourist calendar will show, have been attached to houses in New England for centuries. They are large structures but act as simple backgrounds for their more delicate, ornate master houses. They are led by the houses in the same way that the large domestic animals they

Figure 2. Rendering of the addition to the Lewis Walpole Library.
Centerbrook Architects and Planners, LLP.

Figure 3. Model of the addition to the Lewis Walpole Library.
Centerbrook Architects and Planners, LLP.

Figure 4. The Lewis Walpole Library from Main Street, Farmington.
Peter Aaron © Esto.

sheltered were led by humans. Barns can also create appealing outdoor spaces. At the Walpole the new barn helps in establishing a courtyard with the two houses and a new miniature orchard designed by our skilled landscape architects, Stephen Stimson and Associates [figs. 2–3]. While this courtyard references the farmyard, it does different work by creating a central campus quadrangle that is crossed by researchers and staff during the day. It hosts celebrations and offers a place to enjoy the view and relax. The courtyard also collects the various Lewis Walpole buildings around it, declaring that they are part of a community. The place thus becomes an institution, while the domestic buildings retain their individual characteristics [fig. 4].

ORGANIZING A FRAMEWORK

The conflicting dicta to make the library both accessible and secure demanded careful organization of the Cowles House and the barn. In our earlier workshops we determined that it was best to have one primary access for both staff and visitors. A series of organizing charts and much consultation helped us establish the location for this new entrance. The single entry would lead to a reception area. From there people needed access to the library's many spaces: the reading room, the New Library, the Cowles House, gallery, classroom, offices, the conservation space, and secure shelving and storage. It was important to move the right people gracefully to the right places while keeping them away from the wrong ones.

Figure 5. The new doorway and passageway. *Peter Aaron © Esto*.

Figure 6. New reception area. *Peter Aaron © Esto*.

An important first step was to create a new front door that would not offend the Cowles House, and we decided that a low connector between the house and barn would establish a respectful space between them. Entering here would lead a visitor to either part of the library. After a few false starts (one was inspired by Greek Revival; our clients appropriately forbade it on this eighteenth-century house), we settled on a design inspired by extraordinary entryways found in Farmington. The new doorway is also an homage to the delicacy and reverse taper columns of the Cowles House porch, an early example of an eighteenth-century American veranda [fig. 5].

We planned the connector to be the spine of the new complex. It houses

Figure 7. New reading room. *Peter Aaron © Esto*.

the reception area [fig. 6] along with connecting halls and the Librarian's office. The back of this area also leads out through French doors to one of the two court gardens, one rebuilt to accommodate the barn. Light floods in from both sides of the connector, making it cheerful and welcoming. To the left of the entry lies the barn, housing the staff and reading room on the first floor and the stacks above and below. The basement stacks are secured from groundwater with "belts and suspenders" waterproofing systems.

The new reading room, a pleasant, harmonious space flooded with indirect daylight, offers careful control of materials and security [fig. 7]. It is organized as a long room with a central table for ten readers. At the head of the room is a higher monitor's desk from which the monitor can keep a watchful eye down the table and on views from discreet security cameras hidden above. The table has sliding counters to separate materials from laptop computers. The walls are lined with varied-depth bookshelves and cabinets for reference works and overnight storage of materials, while the high oak ceilings, patterned with Strawberry Hill Gothic arches, offer light and inspiration.

To the right of the entry is a hall leading to the old house and the twentieth-century storage additions that have been transformed into a gallery and classroom with its own exterior entry. The classroom was the project's lonely stepchild. When the budget got tight it was stripped of all niceties, but we rectified this with a stenciling party after construction. Staff and designers met one afternoon and evening to stencil a frieze across the top of the walls using a pattern based on Gothic shelving in the library at Strawberry Hill.

The gallery, formerly storage space, has been fitted with flexible hanging walls for rotating exhibitions. Track lights can be reconfigured as needed, and central display tables can showcase even the largest folios. Windows can be darkened if the materials demand, and the gallery's location next to the long hall means that exhibitions can expand when required.

The entry to the gallery is located on axis with the new entry hall across the perpendicular "Long Hall," which was the twentieth-century connector from the Cowles House to the New Library. The Long Hall is still used as an informal gallery of paintings, while the New Library is now used by scholars for reading and also for receptions and serves a reminder of the Lewises' legendary hospitality [frontispiece].

The Cowles House, at the other end of the Long Hall, had been preserved as an artifact of twentieth-century habitation of an eighteenth-century house. To rectify the discrepancy, the garage and a small but ungainly twentieth-century addition to the kitchen were demolished. This stripped the exterior of the Cowles House back to its original bones and also opened up the courtyard and made both the old house and new entry more visible.

MAKING A GREAT LIBRARY

While the old library had cramped staff offices spread across the buildings, staff workstations are now grouped together in new offices and facilitate improved communication and collaboration. The offices are carefully laid out to be as efficient as possible while giving staff members the room they need to do their work. Large work tables and intern desks are at the north side, adjacent to the conservation workspace. Flexibility is important because tasks, materials, people, and times all change. Work areas and desks are similar but modular so that jobs and projects can be shared. The conservation space, in an adjacent room with modern environmental controls, features state-of-the-art equipment, including large work areas, paper flotation sink with de-ionized water, and a snorkel hood for ventilation. The space also houses scanning and digitization equipment.

Items in the Lewis Walpole's collection vary dramatically in size, ranging from objects from Strawberry Hill to prints to books of every format. The majority of the collection is now kept in compact stacks with custom shelves. Flat files of prints line one wall of the new collections storage area, while objects occupy their own room. Paintings hang on a museum storage system, and all of these spaces have museum-quality temperature and humidity controls, as do the staff offices, reading room, exhibition gallery, and classroom.

GREENING THE PLACE

Centerbrook and Yale were both determined to make the new Lewis Walpole Library green and sustainable. We wanted to create a healthy, long-lived, and efficient place that would minimize the use of carbon-based energy. One of the first things to consider in making a sustainable building is massing and solar

Figure 8. A view of the barn from the south. *Peter Aaron © Esto.*

exposure. A building in New England wants to gather winter solar heat and natural light while avoiding summer solar heat. Thus the barn's long south-side windows have overhangs that block summer light but let in the rays of the low-lying winter sun [fig. 8]. The east and west sides of the building are shorter, showing less bulk from the street, and are windowless to avoid the summer's long morning and evening sun.

A unique task in designing lighting was to avoid direct and ultraviolet light exposure on the library's rare and sometimes fragile materials. A long dormer in the reading room brings light in from above the arching wood ceiling to bounce evenly across a high wall and then down to the readers below. This also brings in solar winter warmth that is collected in the heating and ventilation return air ducts. A lower run of reading room windows mimics the patterns of local barns and uses blinds to keep out the direct sun while providing scholars with views of the landscape. Glass windows were laminated and treated to reflect ultraviolet rays. All light fixtures use sensors to adjust for brightness depending on the amount of arriving daylight, balancing overall building light levels while also minimizing costs and energy use.

To diminish additional energy needs, all of the new construction is highly insulated with soy-based foam that seals the building against air leaks as well as energy loss. By setting one of the floors of stacks in the ground, almost a third of the new construction enjoys the ground's thermal stability. The ground also offers even more energy through a geothermal heat-pump system. This

Figure 9. The Lewis Walpole Library from the west lawn. *Peter Aaron © Esto.*

heating and cooling approach, invented in the 1940s, is again popular in these sustainable times. While its initial cost is higher than typical heating, ventilation, and cooling systems, it pays for itself in savings over approximately ten years. Two open-loop standing column wells, 1,200 and 1,100 feet, respectively, draw groundwater from below the surface, where its temperature is about fifty-five degrees Fahrenheit year round. Using groundwater as a transfer medium, the deep earth serves as a thermal battery, storing winter cold for summer cooling and summer heat for winter warming. An enthalpy wheel provides heat transfer between fresh air and exhaust air while controlling humidity. Carbon monoxide is monitored in occupied and collection spaces, and elaborate electronic controls manage the entire system to make it as efficient and healthy as possible.

Reusing materials and providing safe and recyclable materials in new construction are both critical to sustainability. Construction debris is the source of a high percentage of American landfills, and contractors on the Walpole project sorted and recycled many of the materials generated through demolition and construction. We were also able to reference the historic nature of the Walpole and its collections in employing recycled materials. Oak used for the flooring in the first-floor hallways, reading room, and exhibition gallery was reclaimed from a ship that sank in the Saint Lawrence River on its way to England during

Horace Walpole's lifetime. The oak was kiln-dried, carefully sawn, and bonded to formaldehyde-free plywood certified by the Forest Stewardship Council. The floor's warm, aged color and finish bring a glow to the day-lit spaces in the new library and provide another connection to Horace Walpole and his times.

Outside, the central court is hard paved to accommodate the handicapped, while the majority of daily parking is on loose gravel to allow rainwater to sink into the ground. Stephen Stimson designed a bioswale next to the barn to collect storm water. This is planted with native species that absorb contaminants before the water continues on to the watershed. It avoids adding to the town of Farmington's storm sewer loads while also acting as a low-maintenance, but pleasant, garden.

SATISFACTION

We resolved the Lewis Walpole Library's four completing priorities even though they were not compatible. We protected the extraordinary collections in flexible and conditioned storage spaces. We made them more accessible to staff, scholars, and the public in a secure reading room, gallery, and classroom, each designed to accommodate a different kind of visitor. We protected and preserved the Cowles House while making it more accessible. Despite the project's conflicting demands, the whole has become a resonant setting, a welcoming and comfortable library that should inspire scholars for generations. The place has unity despite its centrifugal needs.

Centerbrook Architects and Planners has done a wide variety of projects over the past thirty-five years, but the Lewis Walpole Library stands as a favorite. It is many things at once: an important research library, a carefully preserved space with a sympathetic and complementary addition, an example of sustainable architecture and landscaping, and an important landmark in Farmington that projects a unique and singular character [fig. 9].

Frontispiece. Engraving of the choir screen from Sir William Dugdale's *History of St. Paul's Cathedral in London . . . Beautified with sundry prospects of the church, figures of tombes, and monuments.*

MARGARET K. POWELL

Twice Borrowed: The Arches and Pinnacles of Strawberry Hill

When Horace Walpole began to turn Strawberry Hill, his house in Twickenham outside London, into a "little gothic castle," one of his first projects was to build a library. Its design was a joint effort by the friends who formed his "Strawberry Committee" and was completed by the end of 1754.[1] Writing to the artist and draftsman Richard Bentley (d. 1782), a member of the Committee, in December 1754, Walpole exulted, "My present occupation is putting up my books; and thanks to arches, and pinnacles, and pierced columns, I shall not appear scantily provided!"

Strawberry Hill is full of inspired borrowings—some from books and engravings, some perhaps from Walpole's visual memory of architectural elements from his visits to the ancient buildings he admired. At least one engraving from one of Walpole's many books, Sir William Dugdale's 1658 *History of St. Paul's Cathedral in London . . . Beautified with sundry prospects of the church, figures of tombes, and monuments* [frontispiece], provided inspiration for the bookshelves designed for Strawberry Hill's library by Walpole's friend John Chute (1701–1776), an architect and the third member of the Committee. A note from Walpole identifying a sketch by Chute says as much: "one side of the library at Strawberry Hill, taken from a doorcase in Dugdale's old St Paul's by Mr Chute."[2] Further evidence of a connection is found in the copy of the book at the Vyne, John Chute's house: the section of the engraving showing the St. Paul's door case has been cut out.

Continuing in the spirit of the original design of Strawberry Hill, it is entirely fitting that Mark Simon and his colleagues at Centerbrook Architects did some borrowing of their own in the design for the renovation and addition to Yale's Lewis Walpole Library. The glorious new reading room's wooden-slatted ceiling features cut-out shapes of arches and quatrefoils, and those elements were also used in the front panel of the monitor's station and in the table supports [fig. 6]. These motifs appear again in friezes, in the protective enclosure housing the Beauclerk Cabinet from Strawberry Hill [fig. 5], and in the entrance ceiling to the reading room. The doors to the reading room, the Librarian's office, and the exhibition space all incorporate a design from a screen in the Holbein Chamber at Strawberry Hill, which, Walpole wrote, was in part taken by Committee member Bentley from "the gates of the choir of Rouen."[3]

After the official opening of the Lewis Walpole Library's new addition in September 2007, Mark Simon had a proposal: he suggested stenciling a design around the top of the newly refurbished classroom to add interest [fig. 7]. Centerbrook would provide the design, teach the art of stenciling, and join us for a stenciling party at the end of a workday. I was to provide a willing staff,

Figure 1. Richard Bentley's design for a "Screen in the Holbein-chamber at Strawberry Hill," mounted in Walpole's *Drawings and Designs by Richd. Bentley*.

and pizza. The design we all enthusiastically stenciled on the classroom walls was taken by the architects from the Strawberry Hill Library's bookshelves, the very "arches and pinnacles" in which Walpole had rejoiced, now twice borrowed.

The illustrations that accompany this essay are taken from books, drawings, and prints in the collection of the Lewis Walpole Library, unless otherwise noted.

NOTES

1. See Walpole's letters to Horace Mann, December 1, 1754, in *Horace Walpole's Correspondence with Sir Horace Mann*, IV, ed. W. S. Lewis, Warren Hunting Smith, and George L. Lam, *The Yale Edition of Horace Walpole's Correspondence*, vol. 20 (New Haven, CT: Yale University Press, 1960), 456; and to Richard Bentley, December 24, 1754, in *Horace Walpole's Correspondence with John Chute, Richard Bentley*, ed. W. S. Lewis, A. Dayle Wallace, and Robert A. Smith, *Walpole's Correspondence*, vol. 35 (New Haven, CT: Yale University Press, 1973), 200.

2. Chute's sketch is in a volume of his drawings kept by Walpole in the Glass Closet and then moved, probably in 1790, to what became a print room in the Round Tower (Hazen 3490). The title, written in Walpole's hand on the flyleaf, is *Slight Sketches of Architecture by John Chute Esq. of the Vine in Hampshire*. We do not know the present location of Walpole's copy of Dugdale's *History of St. Paul's*, but we do know that there was a copy at Chute's house in Basingstoke, with one of Walpole's bookplates inserted. See entry 591 in Allen T. Hazen, *A Catalogue of Horace Walpole's Library*, with Wilmarth Sheldon Lewis, *Horace Walpole's Library*, 3 vols. (New Haven, CT: Yale University Press, 1969).

3. Horace Walpole, *A Description of the Villa of Mr. Horace Walpole: Youngest Son of Sir Robert Walpole Earl of Orford at Strawberry-Hill at Twickenham, Middlesex. With an inventory of the furniture, pictures, curiosities, &c.* (Strawberry Hill: Printed by Thomas Kirgate, 1784), 43. Walpole wrote and had printed at his own Strawberry Hill Press a detailed description of his house and its contents, first in 1774 and then, with additions, in 1784.

Figure 2. Etching and engraving of the realized "Screen of the Holbein Chamber" from Walpole's extra-illustrated copy of *A Description of the Villa of Horace Walpole*.

Figure 3. "The Library at Strawberry Hill," etching and engraving by Richard Bernard Godfrey, in *A Description of the Villa of Horace Walpole*.

Figure 4. The Library at Strawberry Hill photographed in 2005 before the start of a restoration program being overseen by the Strawberry Hill Trust.
Richard Holltum.

Figure 5. Arches and quatrefoils are repeated again in the new case designed to house and protect the Beauclerk Cabinet.
The Lewis Walpole Library.

Figure 6. The new reading room at the Lewis Walpole Library. Its wooden-slatted ceiling, table, and monitor's desk feature cut-out shapes of arches and quatrefoils borrowed from the design and decoration of Strawberry Hill.
Peter Aaron © Esto.

Figure 7. The design of the stencil used to decorate the Lewis Walpole Library's new classroom was based on the bookcases at Strawberry Hill.
Centerbrook Architects and Planners, LLP.

Frontispiece. Plan and elevation drawing of the Bass Library entry pavilion.
The inscription reads: "A beautiful thing is forever a source of delight."
Aric Lasher/Hammond Beeby Rupert Ainge (HBRA).

ARIC LASHER

Cathedral, Cloister, Crypt: Bass and the Evolution of the Yale Library

The recontextualization of Cross Campus Library as the Anne T. and Robert M. Bass Library afforded a unique opportunity to consider the transformation of the university library in an age of digital information. An essential objective of this undertaking was to retain the representational role and architectural character of the library at Yale and its place within an architectural program thoroughly enmeshed with Yale's status and identity. The library beneath the Cross Campus lawn remained essentially unchanged since opening in 1970 and suffered from programmatic obsolescence and extensive structural and systemic flaws. Cross Campus Library's character, condition, and configuration presented significant challenges in adapting the existing underground structure to incorporate a modern, flexible program in a building that would assert a distinct identity within a context of notable architectural richness.

The history of the Yale Library as told by the buildings that have housed its collections offers a compelling reflection on Yale's institutional culture and its relationship to broader trends and agendas in architecture and the design of college campuses. The first building constructed specifically to serve as Yale's library was Henry Austin's College Library, built in 1846 in an ecclesiastical, perpendicular Gothic style in a central location on campus. Upon its abandonment with the moving of books to its successor, James Gamble Rogers's Sterling Memorial Library, it was converted to serve as a chapel, a fitting end for a building whose resemblance to a church lent prestige and specific honorific association to the role of the Library within the University. The status of the library as a central, sacred, and hierarchically privileged edifice within the Yale campus remained intact until the expansion of the Sterling Memorial Library in the early 1970s, when a new facility beneath the Cross Campus green introduced a functionalist-modernist approach to the planning and architectural expression of the university library.

The plan to construct a new and larger facility for the collections that would replace the original College Library followed the receipt of a substantial legacy in 1918 from the estate of John W. Sterling for unspecified campus construction. Architect John Russell Pope's subsequent 1919 plan for campus expansion positioned a new library near the space now occupied by Beinecke Plaza and presupposed the demolition of the Commons. At this time, Cross Campus did not yet exist and was not, in its current state, part of Pope's plan. Following publication, Pope's plan was evaluated by a trio of architects that included Bertram Grosvenor Goodhue, who was eventually awarded the library commission, to be built on the site now occupied by Sterling. Goodhue's initial designs embraced a range of expressive approaches, from the Gothic to the classical, but upon his death in 1924 the commission was transferred to James Gamble Rogers, architect of the Memorial Quadrangle and a critic of Goodhue's earlier schemes.[1]

Rogers developed a comprehensive plan for campus expansion, placing the new Sterling Memorial Library in a position of authority within a unified ensemble of colleges and university buildings that extended the idiom first introduced through his design for the original Memorial Quadrangle and effectively shifted the center of the University from the Old Campus.[2] The location, expression, and organization of Sterling perpetuate the notion of the Library as the exalted heart of the University and do so in a manner specific to Yale.

The Rogers campus buildings established a compelling narrative for Yale as an intricate labyrinth that alternately conceals and exposes moments of architectural revelation that might be intimate or grand, but always memorable. Prior to the building campaign of the 1920s and 1930s, the campus lacked a specific and unified architectural character, and the expansion not only accommodated a change in Yale's institutional structure but also produced a unique and totalizing environment whose presence was particularly effective in inspiring allegiance to the university whose identity it embodied. This Oxfordian fabric was wrought from materials chosen for their characteristic texture and capacity to demonstrate antique qualities straight out of the box. The seam-faced granite and porous sandstone provided a ready-patinated tapestry that quickly absorbed the soot of soft coal and whose profiles eroded in short time, evoking venerability and the charm of wear. Rogers's ensembles were woven together with banding, scrolls, and picturesque compositional events and transitions that lent them the heterogeneous cohesion of a coral reef. The embroidery of these buildings, inside and out, with conventionalized architectural elements from various periods, narrative sculpture and reliefs, tablets with phrases and the names of historic figures, and a proliferation of foliated ornamentation produced an extraordinarily beguiling setting for the veneration of inquiry. The deeply affecting experience of these spaces and elements over time is remarkable for the imprint with which it leaves the visitor, and its power as a manifestation and tool of the *Alma Mater* fosters a profound allegiance among its alumni. Like the Gothic cathedral, the value of this group of buildings as a mechanism of persuasion and indoctrination is undeniable. Subsequent digressions from the core principles of Rogers's campus design failed to diminish the role that this coordinated ensemble plays in defining Yale's presence in the public imagination and the memory of its students.

Sterling occupies a central position within this arrangement, and its mass dominates the turrets, towers, and crenellations of its neighbors. The library is internally organized about a central nave whose plan and architectural elements are unapologetically derived from those of a cathedral. Its reading rooms and courtyards are richly embellished and were contrived to recall monastery cloisters, refectories, and private clubs. Its essential qualities have been likened to those of a vast, domestic interior, and the variety of spaces, their arrangement, and

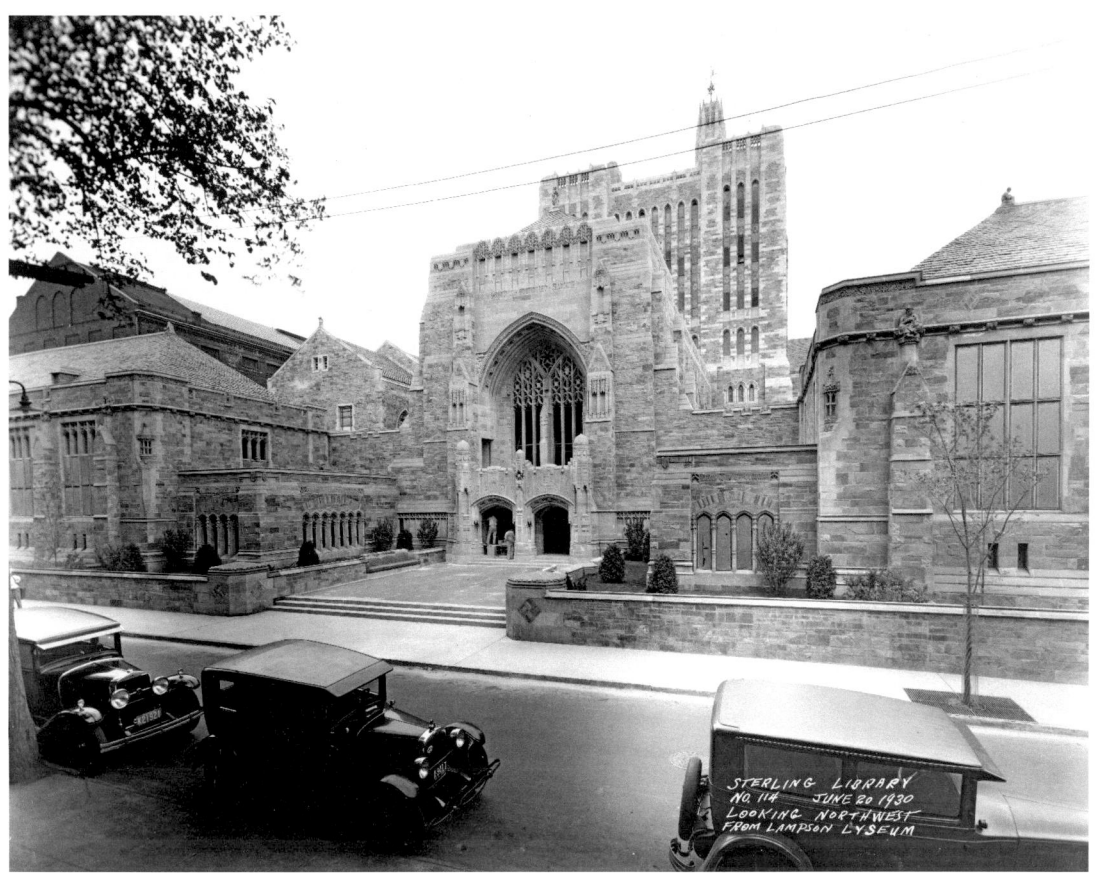

Figure 1. Sterling Memorial Library from High Street, June 1930.
Sterling Memorial Library, Yale University, Photographs (RU 696).
Manuscripts and Archives, Yale University Library.

the intimacy of their experience are distinctly non-institutional.[3] The dominant impression of Sterling is one of representational grandeur, and as such Sterling demonstrates a triumphant expansion of the notion of library as the cathedral to the university's city first and modestly suggested in the old College Library.

A highly specialized arrangement of program elements and supporting spaces, Sterling belies rather than expresses its operational complexity. The organization of the library was sophisticated, functionally robust, and successfully addressed the programmatic demands of what was one of the world's largest research libraries while advancing the narrative of Yale's campus as an enveloping vessel charged with meaning. Sterling's exterior, as seen from Cross Campus, presents an image evocative of a cathedral's portal, but it is perhaps more remarkable for its often overlooked abstract characteristics. The entrance face of Sterling reconciles the picturesque domesticity of adjoining colleges with its monumental interior through the subtle manipulation of scale achieved by compositional massing and carefully considered application of ornamentation [fig. 1]. The entry is unexpectedly diminutive when approached, and the ornamental program of the doorway ensemble is so abstracted from the Gothic as to be more specifically allied with the eclectic and attenuated "skyscraper style" of the 1920s. The stacks tower on the York Street side is nearly bereft of elaboration and, apart from its fanciful skyline of lead-clad penthouses, expresses the presence of a utilitarian, self-supporting stacks assembly within, characterized by Kent Bloomer, designer, sculptor, and adjunct professor in the Yale School of Architecture, as "an engine room of books."[4] As realized, the library bears little specific resemblance to any orthodox model of academic or ecclesiastical architecture, but instead uses fragments episodically to construct a convincing persona for the institution.

The richness of execution achieved at Sterling was reinforced by a program of ornamentation and decorative elaboration that supported its representational identity as a cathedral of knowledge, the acquisition of which has been elevated to a devotional ritual through association and ornamental depiction [fig. 2]. Carved reliefs in the nave describe the transfer of books to an earlier Yale library, and a ceremonial procession commemorated this event with the installation of significant volumes at the dedication of Sterling. In his definitive work *The Nature of Ornament* (2000), Kent Bloomer examines Sterling's appropriation of familiar motifs and their application in the service of assignment of meaning to the building within the culture of the University. Bloomer asserts that, like a cathedral, the building is to be read as a book, and the impression one is left with establishes Yale and the endeavor of study within an extensive continuum of culture and memory.[5] Its pervasive themes address books, reading, and scholarship, and as such reiterate Sterling's place within an exceptional constellation.

Reaction to the new library was not entirely enthusiastic, and challenges to the architectural orthodoxy that Sterling was seen to personify were being advanced by the promise of a new architectural language. The subsequent postwar abandonment of the Collegiate Gothic program was both ideological and economic in origin, and the promise of new materials, methods, and modes of expression prevailed over the adaptation and extension of earlier models for new academic buildings. The hegemonic success of modernism was followed by the general establishment of a clear boundary behind which worthy artifacts from earlier times were to be preserved while new additions stood apart in autonomous opposition. The Beinecke Rare Book and Manuscript Library, designed by Gordon Bunshaft of Skidmore, Owings and Merrill and completed in 1963, marked a dramatic departure from prior assumptions regarding the notion of a Yale library building of exceptional stature.[6] However, it still managed to satisfy the expectations that would be placed on an edifice conceived to house Yale's legacy of extraordinary volumes, albeit through an unfamiliar idiom. Texts and collections formerly contained in Sterling's chapel-like Rare Book Room and elsewhere were consolidated, mostly below grade and out of sight, but the prestige of the Beinecke within the precinct of the Bicentennial Buildings is most dramatically stated by the obfuscating monumentality of its marble-enclosed sanctum. Like Sterling, Beinecke is a hallowed treasure-box, but, appropriately, architecturally and programmatically hermetic. The model of an essentially invisible

Figure 2. A view into Sterling Memorial Library's Sellin Courtyard from the exhibit corridor. *Amanda Patrick*.

subterranean complex identified by an honorific presence above avoided the difficulties of introducing a substantial, alien, and largely opaque structure into a constellation of diminutive and highly elaborate buildings, and the library enshrines its collections within a convincingly nontraditional evocation of its classical neighbors. The hushed sanctity of its mezzanine conjures a Byzantine richness that serves as a dramatic foil to the bronze and glass reliquaries of which the central stacks tower is but the largest. Through modern means, the library manages to assume the stature and awe-inspiring gravity of sacred architecture, and its placement alongside adjacent buildings of classical derivation suggests deference as much as opposition. Like all distinctly Yale buildings, the library conceals and unveils remarkable architectural rewards. In an ineffable twist on the tradition of Rogers's Yale, Beinecke Library successfully conveys its privileged status with a monumental presence, the substitution of a significant art installation for ornamental splendor, a materials palette of extraordinary richness, and an extensive array of custom-designed and fabricated furnishings and fittings. While oppositional in its rejection of historical precedent, Beinecke dutifully fulfills the role of a Yale building through a memorable and evocative spatial experience, material excellence, and iconic stature, while its embrace of an exotic representational spirit sets it apart from the more widely endorsed canon of American modernism.

Finding space to house Sterling's expanding collections in the late 1960s proved difficult as the environment adjacent to Cross Campus allowed little room for substantial growth. The desire for increased access to a core collection as well as additional open and individual study areas within a limiting architectural ensemble was especially challenging. The Collegiate Gothic idiom of Sterling and Berkeley College had become economically unfeasible and was ideologically prohibited within the contemporary architectural community. A subterranean expansion beneath the Cross Campus green addressed these challenges, and the intervention was ultimately unobtrusive and deferential. Similar strategies were later employed later by Gunnar Birkerts, a protégé of Eero Saarinen, for underground library expansions at the University of Michigan and Cornell University, and they were effective, if perhaps aesthetically lacking, in preserving the architectural integrity of the older progenitors through isolation and opposition rather than extension.[7] Initial design proposals for Cross Campus Library (CCL) had skylights penetrating the lawn above, but these were ultimately abandoned, vindicating community outrage over these intrusions with a dialed-down scheme with little presence above.

The architectural strategy for CCL was influenced as much by economics as by ethos. The new building provided many square feet while avoiding the staggering expense that a true, above-grade Collegiate Gothic building would require. The broadly sanctioned approach that married minimalism and functionalism conveniently accommodated circumstance, and the arrangement of two relatively unelaborated pancakes of space beneath a carpet of grass was nothing if not anti-Rogers and modest. The moments at which CCL asserted any qualitative identity were to be found at its sunken courtyards, with two larger ones at the west side serving as entry points and others providing windows and a necessary means of egress. Here, the supporting earth was peeled away, floating weightless above uninterrupted ribbons of glass. Inside, the unencumbered open spaces of the stacks and study areas were encircled by two-person study rooms, all rendered in white laminate with evenly distributed fluorescent lighting fixtures fastened to a plane of acoustic tile. As a complement to Sterling, CCL was experienced not as a collection of honorific spaces with distinct characteristics but rather as an ambivalent open space with functional zones and elements floating within. Surfaces were unarticulated and materials were modest, even rudimentary. The heart of the library was not an open space used to orient the user but rather a solid zone of fully enclosed support areas around which patrons could wander. The oppositional character of the new library was evident in the use of what might otherwise be considered traditional materials at the courtyards, where CCL's cool limestone walls engaged Berkeley's warm-hued granite and sandstone. A material foreign to Cross Campus was used in a texture-less, nonstructural manner for ends entirely opposite to those of Rogers's campus.

CCL offered a striking alternative to those unmoved by Sterling's textured grandiloquence. The shortcomings of the building that became evident over time, however, were both structural and architectural, and the minimalist presence that preserved the green above did not serve Sterling as successfully. The configuration of the two courtyards as points of entry proved a security challenge, and one was abandoned while the other was provided an accessible entrance via elevator that intruded on the plaza above with a freestanding pavilion. Original Rogers garden pavilions in the courtyards of Berkeley North and South had been converted to mechanical intakes and exhausts, and were conspicuously disfigured. Nontraditional detailing of stone parapets and window walls led to water infiltration and undesired staining, compromising their pristine appearance [fig. 3]. A stair introduced in the center of the Sterling nave to provide access to the new building was minimal in its aesthetic, but as a foreign intervention was disruptive to what was the library's most significant space. This stair led to a basement-level vending area that brought the spare aesthetic of CCL to the doorstep of the nave and was in turn connected to the new library by a sloping tunnel ending in a half-level stair that made wheelchair access problematic. The lower level of CCL's two floors was lightly used due to its lack of natural light, and access was inconvenient as it was served only by emergency exits and diminutive stairways nearly hidden within the building's core. Over time, leaks appeared in the roof and courtyards, the mechanical system proved inadequate, and the accommodation of computers, power, and data connections was limited and provisional. Addressing these issues provided an opportunity to introduce programmatic innovations to the library, and the University enlisted the services of an architectural firm to investigate possible directions for

Figure 3. View into the north west courtyard of the former Cross Campus Library. *HBRA*.

its renovation. The ensuing evaluation would test the validity of CCL's premise of a Yale library as laboratory rather than cathedral-manor house. Structural and mechanical systems could be improved; however, CCL, with its lack of mystery and meaning, had failed to engender a degree of affection or status that would ensure its preservation along the lines of its original architectural intentions.

Hammond Beeby Rupert Ainge Architects was entrusted with the design of the renovations in 2006–07, following conclusion of the initial study. While its recommendations included a revised functional program, the study's architectural conclusions were unresolved, and subsequently, a range of organizational strategies was developed by HBRA. Essential objectives of all approaches included establishment of a legible internal organization and strengthened relationship to Sterling to address the jarring schism below the nave and the disorienting arrangement of spaces within CCL. Accommodation of digital media and improved mechanical services would be uniformly distributed in such a way as to allow for later flexibility and the eventual incorporation of new technologies and enhancements. Programmatic innovations, including group study rooms, technology consulting areas, individual study rooms, and a café, would compensate for deficiencies of Sterling's older operational model and thereby enhance interaction between the two libraries. With an expanded program and measures to make the building a more accessible and desirable destination, the library would pursue a more robust engagement with Cross Campus and the broader Yale environment.

An overall organization along a central axis was adopted, and a general, symmetrical distribution of elements to either side of this spine effectively compensated for the disorienting aspects of a large and relatively windowless underground building. This linear west-to-east arrangement originates beneath Sterling's nave, where the former location of "Machine City" was to be converted to an ensemble of a central study lounge flanked by new restrooms and a trio of seminar rooms. Access from the nave would be provided by a stair that would take the place of a former cloak room beyond one of the archivolts of the south wall, which had since been converted to offices [figs. 4–5]. The existing stair element would be removed and the nave floor restored, allowing for a more serviceable arrangement of spaces below.

The architectural sequence from Sterling to CCL would be enhanced and reinforced. The existing tunnel would be shortened, with the intervening space between its termination and the new building occupied by a monumental stair that incorporated an elevator at its landings for wheelchair access and book cart movement between the two libraries. This circulation armature would achieve a clearly visible, honorific connection to CCL's formerly orphaned lower level. Courtyards would no longer be points of entry but rather secured, dedicated light-courts for adjacent lounge areas and individual study rooms that could be used as outdoor reading areas. The extension of the spine toward the east, through an area formerly occupied by offices and service rooms, would now present a clear and direct path from the tunnel landing and courtyard reading area, between the circulation desk and collections area, and terminate in a study lounge with café just beyond the security boundary of the library. This path would incorporate additional broad, communicating stairways, mitigating the segregation of the lower level that had rendered half of the library less than useful. The café lounge would allow casual study and social interaction and provide access at both of its ends to Cross Campus above. The new library would now have as its vestibule an amenity that could mediate between the public realm of the campus and the private realm of the library. The processional spine, easily navigated and intuitively apparent, would impart architectural legibility—an arrangement that was self-explanatory and allowed for the simple disposition of what would be a complex assortment of spaces in size and function. Its clear origin, orientation, path, and termination would link the reconfigured library to the coinciding axis of the nave and principal spaces of Sterling above, and as such it would become part of an integrated, cohesive ensemble. Rather than asserting its otherness from Sterling and the green, the reconsidered library would now achieve a unified gradation of program from public to private, exterior to interior.

This rational planning strategy served to inform all subordinate systems and arrangements. Program elements to be accommodated ranged from individual study rooms to intimate group-study rooms, classrooms of various sizes, lounge areas, and technology-rich instruction spaces and consulting areas. Rather than enclosing each space in a discrete and hierarchical fashion, as found in premodern university buildings, the open-plan strategy of the original building was elaborated upon and transformed. A regular matrix of structural bays could be

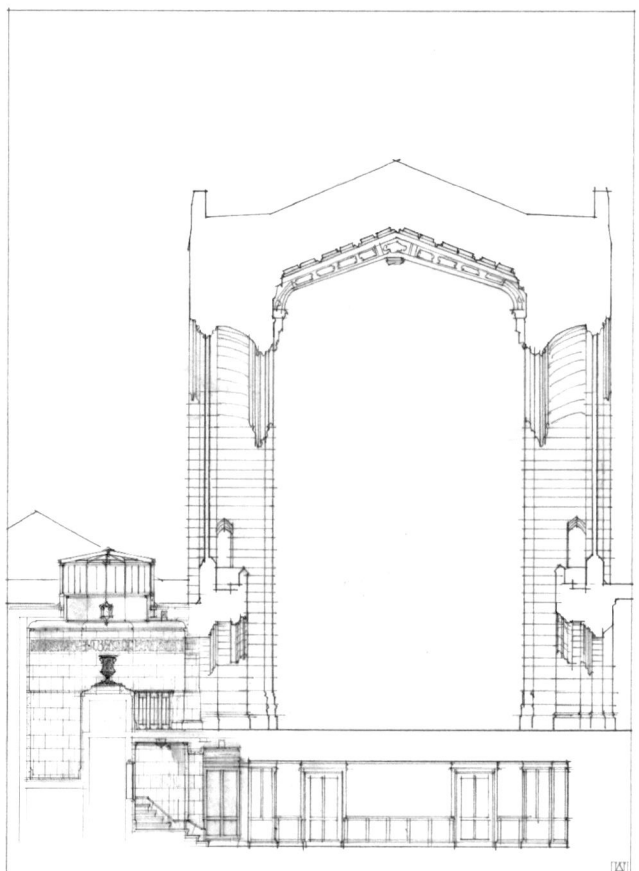

Figure 4. Design phase section drawing showing the Sterling nave, a new stair, and lower-level study area, later named the Wright Reading Room. *Aric Lasher/HBRA.*

populated with spaces of varying degrees of enclosure, access, visual continuity, and acoustic isolation while maintaining a clear and unifying order over which the sequence along the central axis could be superimposed. As such, the reconfigured library can be seen as a hybrid of its modernist predecessor and more spatially diverse buildings like Sterling, unencumbered by both the limitations imposed by CCL's general spatial continuity as well as the specificity and inflexibility of earlier planning conventions. This approach lent itself to working within the confines of a building envelope that provided neither opportunity for sectional elaboration nor perimeter expansion and suggests a conceptual transparency that avoids the claustrophobia that fully enclosed subterranean rooms can induce. Some relief from relentless horizontality would be afforded through introduction of two-story-high spaces at the north and south walls of the building. These glass-enclosed group-study rooms provide a visual link between the two floors of the library and clearly delineate the library's enclosing walls. Proposed skylights to bring daylight to the lower level at these locations would have required modification of the Berkeley garden walls and the narrowing of Cross Campus, and they were ultimately rejected on the same grounds as Edward Larrabee Barnes's unrealized penetrations of the lawn.

A new connection to the campus above through the café vestibules to the east and the redesign of the former ramp and stair configuration at Sterling

Figure 5. A new top-lit stair leads from the Sterling nave to the Wright Reading Room and the tunnel to the Bass Library. The ornamental sandstone frieze of books and vines was designed by Kent Bloomer and realized using a combination of robot milling and hand carving. *Timothy Hursley*.

allow for an enhanced aboveground presence for the library as well as the remediation of some of the intrusive and ad hoc encumbrances visited upon Cross Campus. Elevator access was relocated to the café end of the building and allowed for the removal of the incongruous pavilion opposite Maya Lin's *Women's Table* on Rose Walk. The new pavilion, courtyards, and stairs to the café below announce the library's presence along the important pedestrian route between the Commons and the Old Campus that crosses Wall and Elm Streets. The integration of mechanical intakes and vents into the courtyard walls enabled reconstruction of the Berkeley garden pavilions, thereby restoring Cross Campus to something closer to its originally intended appearance.

The strategic revision of CCL sought to redress several of those characteristics that intentionally and unintentionally disengaged the library from Cross Campus, Sterling, and the expectations placed upon a Yale library. This process did not seek to simply revive an earlier design methodology or aesthetic vocabulary. The redesigned building is modern in its planning approach and spatial ordering, and its exploitation of symmetry is more closely allied with the work of Ludwig Mies van der Rohe than that of James Gamble Rogers.[8] It is in its material expression that the new building most intimately embraces the idea of mythical Yale and as such could be superficially misconstrued as a historical or revivalist work. The serious engagement of nuanced architectural expression and exploration of its meanings and methods with regard to this specific campus was a critical component of the development of the design for the library.

With a strategic organization agreed upon, the architects next explored alternative versions for the material realization of the building and how such approaches would position it within a physical realm and institutional memory. As part of this process, several distinct approaches were devised and described through a series of perspective and elevation drawings that depicted the entry pavilions at the east end of the building within the setting of Cross Campus, each eponymously titled with its defining architectural material. The design of the pavilion was fundamental in that it would ultimately establish an identity for the library and would suggest a direction for the development of its interior architectural systems.

The "glass" proposal was self-effacing, though materially and qualitatively elevated from the modest minimalism of the original Cross Campus Library [fig. 6]. This approach suggested an extension of the expressive strategy adopted by Barnes for CCL, which sought near-invisibility through simplification of building profile and reduction of building mass. The glass pavilion demonstrated an absence of historically derived elements, but respected its neighbors through formal isolation and adopted the modernist program of a free and unencumbered expression with an evocation of newness that would also speak to the history of the original building. The pavilion was to be supported by minimal profiles seen on edge or bias, rather like the legs of Mies' glass-topped tables. The structural frame would be sheathed in bronze and enclosed with glass, and through reduction of apparent surface and mass and use of reflective materials would stand delicately apart from its massive neighbors.

The "metal" scheme was interpretive, taking as its point of departure the Noah Porter Gate found at the south end of the Cross Campus precinct on Elm Street between Berkeley and Calhoun Colleges [fig. 7]. This scheme adapted the brick and stone vocabulary of the gate's Georgian masonry piers for its enclosed and primary structural components. Secondary elements would be rendered in steel and cast iron to recall the qualities and silhouette of the gates and grillage of Samuel Yellin's extraordinary metalsmithy. A variation on this approach, the "brick" scheme, offered a more specifically Georgian language and, like the "metal" scheme, followed the premise of extending the vocabulary of the freestanding brick and stone gate piers to comprise a distinct family of elements that would inhabit the swath of space that cleaves Cross Campus and terminates at Beinecke Plaza [fig. 8]. A fourth approach, "stone," adopted the Collegiate Gothic vocabulary of the surrounding buildings and included a pair of symmetrical pavilions to serve as large-scaled gate posts for a precinct that through extension of its axis and idiom would reinforce the domination of Sterling over this western portion of the Cross Campus green [fig. 9].

The direction ultimately selected endorsed a Collegiate Gothic vocabulary for those portions of the building that had an aboveground presence on Cross

Campus. This approach suggested a general character for the library's underground components, but their subterranean aspect allowed for a departure from what would be considered a conventional expression of a Collegiate Gothic building. The conceit devised for the building was that of an undercroft or cellar for Sterling's cathedral and the ensemble of buildings above. This called for not the typical plastered and paneled halls of a building like Sterling, but rather a more substantial and utilitarian fabric appropriate to a medieval basement or fortification. In this way, the library now extends its historical association with sacred architecture while allowing for an expression appropriate to the support of an earthen roof free from specific features characteristic of Sterling or familiar devotional spaces. The relationship defined by the original Cross Campus Library, in which orientation to the Rogers buildings was established through inversion of their architectural character, was again reversed. The existing structural grid of visually insubstantial concrete columns was encased in masonry and joined by a network of millwork beams that together define an open matrix that could be enclosed as needed. A system of shallow ceiling vaults was adopted for open areas flanking the central spine of the building, which when integrated with a system of slotted, expressed beams concealed mechanical ducts and provided spatial uplift by recalling a structural silhouette characteristic of traditional below-grade construction. The materials chosen comprise a palette of brick and stone found within the vicinity of Cross Campus, and woodwork finish was achieved through a modified replication of the process originally specified by Rogers for the limed oak panels at Sterling. The ceiling grid was conceived as the sectional equivalent of the planning grid, and beams were designed to receive partitions, support vaults, or surround filled coffers to accommodate mechanical services where these were necessary [fig. 10]. This explicit assignment and expression of architectural systems identifies Bass as a modern building, but, as was the case with the pavilion, the development of a transitional grammar and palette for these elements allowed for the new building's integration with its non-modern neighbors.

Infill partitions were intended to appear substantial but distinctly non-structural, inhabiting the space between static masonry piers. The profile and articulation of their panels recall those used by Rogers elsewhere on campus, but their simplified divisions and attenuated proportions support a rhythmic and proportional motif that is repeated throughout the new building. These partitions can be removed or relocated along other grid lines if needed, providing a system that allows for future reconfiguration without extensive reconstruction or remodeling. The system's components include solid panels, glazed window panels, book stack end panels, doors, and roll-up gate enclosures. The design of these walls reconciles irregularities resulting from off-module room sizes or variations within the existing structural grid through subtle adjustment of panel spacing.

A defining element within the new building was retained from the "metal" scheme and further developed as a system of glazed screens that could alternately

Figure 6. The pavilion as shown in the "glass" proposal. This scheme extended CCL's original strategy through simplification of the building profile and use of transparent and reflective materials. *Aric Lasher/HBRA*.

Figure 7. The "metal" scheme adapted the vocabulary and materials of the nearby Noah Porter Gate to establish an intermediate range of related elements along the path from Old Campus to Beinecke Plaza. *Aric Lasher/HBRA*.

Figure 8. The "brick" scheme was a variation of the "metal" proposal with a more specifically Georgian vocabulary. *Aric Lasher/HBRA*.

Figure 9. The "stone" proposal adopted the Collegiate Gothic idiom and characteristic materials of neighboring buildings. *Aric Lasher/HBRA*.

Figure 10. The Thain Family Café, showing characteristic arrangement of ceiling vaults, masonry piers, and glazed screens. *Timothy Hursley*.

serve as exterior window-walls or enclosing partitions to provide acoustic separation and secure boundaries while allowing for visual continuity and light penetration [fig. 11]. These vertically proportioned steel window grids with applied castings and profiles reiterate the attenuated rhythmic verticality of their Gothic neighbors as well as the gates, grillwork, and forged fittings found throughout Sterling and its environs, many of which were executed by the workshop of Samuel Yellin and which stand as extraordinary examples of what was a brief but spectacular renaissance of the metalworking craft in the 1920s and 1930s. Sand-cast and rolled elements augment the essential characteristics of these screens, accentuating their verticality and bringing them into a universe that at its most robust includes the stained glass windows and ornamental metalwork of Sterling Memorial Library. These screens support a modernist approach to enclosure and division of space, but they also specifically recall industrial casements and the decorative embellishment of Sterling. They represent a transformational synthesis with multiple architectural readings and roles and participate in a program of enrichment and ornamentation that was implemented to bring Bass into meaningful engagement with its context.

Ornamental enrichment, until its widespread rejection by architects in the twentieth century, was a fundamental component of architectural expression. It was deployed in Rogers's buildings at Yale as a means of making architectural elements more tectonically expressive and better integrated within an overall composition, and it was also a narrative tool exploited to illustrate and describe

Figure 11. View of Bass's north west courtyard from the concourse level study area.
Aric Lasher/HBRA.

the position of the University within its own and broader academic and cultural history. Ornament can be literally read as a text or can, in a more abstract role, make manifest the essential characteristics of an element or ensemble. Modern architecture embraced a notion that the elements of architecture were best presented in their native state and that any grace notes would only obfuscate their true role and essence, while modern methods of construction first industrialized the production of ornament and then eliminated it altogether, occasionally on grounds of its extravagance and costliness. Sterling Memorial Library was developed through application of ornament as the architectural equivalent of an illuminated manuscript, and any attempt to dovetail new additions into this amalgam would have to address this aspect in some way. The modernization or abstraction of the Collegiate Gothic through elimination of this dimension produced unsuccessful versions that lacked the essential qualities of the original and as such discredited the consideration of pre-modern models as a strategy. To integrate Bass into the collegiate fabric of Cross Campus successfully, it was considered imperative that ornamental components be part of the design for elements that directly engaged their neighbors—specifically, the new stair at the Sterling nave and the entry pavilion introduced at Cross Campus.

The design of the Sterling stair and entry pavilion provided clear opportunities for the integration of programmatic ornament. The stair's sandstone frieze terminates the vertical extension of its walls and provides a transition to its skylit lantern. This frieze is visible from within the nave, and an absence of ornament in this heavily enriched context would be unexpected. The entry pavilion's archivolts follow the lead of those that surmount major openings at Sterling and spring from ornamented terminals at their imposts. A carved frieze encircles the pavilion's parapet and originates from an emerging tree motif at the primary arches' apexes. Buttresses develop ornamental crockets at their terminations, and the ridges and intersections of the roof are punctuated with finials and cresting that intertwine its material silhouette with the bright void of the sky in a manner similar to that of Sterling's festive copper-clad turrets [frontispiece]. The generalized elements of crocket terminals, a tree of knowledge, and a plaque with Yale's book, motto ("Lux et Veritas"), and an illuminating torch were proposed for their thematic appropriateness to their subject. Kent Bloomer was enlisted to develop this ornamentation for both his deep understanding of the principles, application, and conventions of ornament as well as his ability to design it in such a way as to fulfill a traditional role without being superficially derivative. Bloomer's extensive knowledge of Yale and the ornamentation of Sterling had been the subject of a chapter in *The Nature of Ornament*, and his familiarity with modern methods of fabrication were essential in realizing such a program within budgetary limits.

The resolution of the motif at the stair frieze allowed for a degree of repetition that provided an economy to offset the cost of specific transitional pieces and the hand-carved finishing of the foliation. This repetition not only suited the metrical nature of the band's design but also allowed the use of robotic carving machinery for the roughing-out of the frieze, a technique that reduced the cost significantly. The foliated scroll and the scalloping of open books echoes motifs found elsewhere in the library, and a related variation whose vines engage a door-lancet crenellation at the pavilion associated the two interventions in character while strengthening the pavilion's identity as a shoot grown up from the extensive roots of Sterling. Stone crockets, book, torch, and owl-and-holly terminals were hand carved, but cast and machined metal roof cresting took advantage of the economy of repetition. The overall appearance of the pavilion as a celebratory and embroidered aedicule identifies it as a point of entry to a significant building and reinforces its alliance with Sterling. The decision to eliminate one of the pair of pavilions respected the subtle asymmetries of the Cross Campus ensemble and diminished the subordination of the remaining pavilion to Sterling's entrance. The pavilion was thereby given a distinct association with Bass and was richly embellished to a degree appropriate to its role as yet another gateway to the University's source of intellectual wealth within its most sacred precinct.

The successful execution of the pavilion relied heavily on the study and application of the specific materials, scale, and configuration of profiles and construction methods found in adjacent buildings. The seam-faced granite surface of the pavilion is particular to Sterling within Cross Campus and thereby identifies the pavilion as part of the library ensemble. The veined Ohio sandstone used for flat and carved elements was quarried from the same source of the original material for the surrounding colleges. Its leaded copper roof and ornaments associate the pavilion thematically with Sterling's embellished skyline, while the descent from Cross Campus to the courtyards below follows a transition of the materials palette and architectural vocabulary from that of the Gothic quadrangle to that of the library below. Brick lining the mouths of the sunken courtyards was chosen to match that found in the inner courts of Berkeley North and South and is used for the structural and enclosing elements of the undercroft. The profiled sandstone capitals of the piers are not specific to any typical Collegiate Gothic expression but serve to relate this supporting foundation to the buildings above. Their interrupted profiles are characteristic of Gothic construction as well as nineteenth-century utilitarian buildings, and the ironwork of the glazed infill recalls both Gothic and early industrial architecture. Passing through the pavilion's vaulted loggia, descending the stair, and crossing the portcullis of the café vestibule screens, a visitor will have been introduced to the formal, material, architectural, and iconographic components that define Bass as a privileged constituent within Cross Campus, an adjunct of Sterling, a supportive substructure for Rogers's ensemble, and a legible assembly of systematized elements that accommodate an innovative array of programmatic entities. It is through these gradations and overlaps that Bass reconciles its more public, utilitarian territory of collaborative study with the exalted realm of the representational library that lies at the opposite end of this sequence.

A considered relationship to the prevailing Yale idiom extends to a coordinated furnishings and decorative arts program conceived for the library. The incorporation of decorative elements and the purposeful design and selection of furniture and fixtures were integral to the design of Rogers's Yale and were similarly essential to the convincing integration of the Bass Library into an environment characterized by persistence of motif and material refinement. These transitional elements supplement the architectural systems to make the building's character and purpose legible to its users and provide the library with a distinct identity. The decorative elements of the building that advance this program include ornamental metalwork and glazing, decorative tile, light fixtures, moveable fixtures, and wall-hung textiles. Custom-designed furnishings bear a specific relationship to architectural systems found in the building, and non-custom furnishings selected for the library were chosen for their compatibility with these elements as well as for their didactic value in representing the transformation and formal innovation that characterized the design of notable furniture in the twentieth century.

A secondary fabric of railings, grilles, and decorative metalwork is woven within the library's masonry frame. Its insistent verticality counters the weighty bearing of the superstructure and suggests a simplified correlative to the leaded casements of Sterling that fill the voids between its piers and tracery. These elements mediate between transparency and opacity, and their silhouette pattern

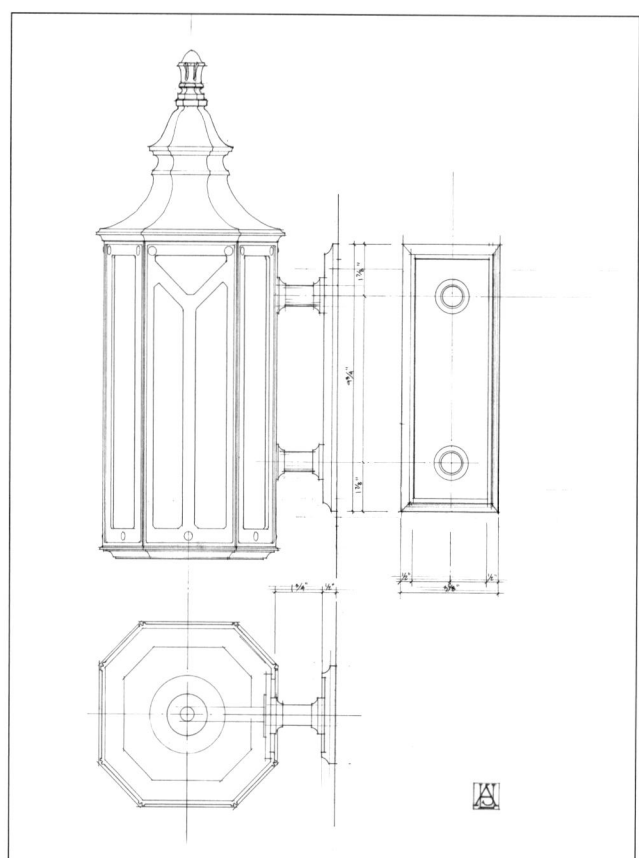

Figure 12. Design drawing for exterior lantern fixtures in Bass's west courtyards. *Aric Lasher/ HBRA.*

divides and subdivides surfaces and views. Leaded transom lights at the upper register of the glazed screens enclosing the café employ materials and motifs found in the wooden screens, transoms, and ornamental door panels of Sterling. Their four-center arches, characteristic of the Collegiate Gothic, reappear in the design of tile and textiles at Bass. Repetition and industrial methods of fabrication and assembly germane to a more utilitarian aesthetic characterize Bass's metalwork, and as such their application is allied to twentieth-century modernism as well as arts and crafts antecedents. Machined and cast elements are more often assembled than forged, but their silhouette and meter are resonant with that of the Yellin gates and grilles nearby. Gates at the lower-level courtyards and cagelike stair grilles at the west stair and tunnel borrow from both the language of the glazed partitions and railings of Bass and the filigree of Yellin's gates at Sterling and Berkeley College. Light fixtures used in exterior settings and transitional spaces such as major stairways and vestibules were designed by the architects specifically for the new library. These lantern fixtures recall historical examples found elsewhere on campus, but their design is decidedly less delicate and employs a vocabulary of elements and motifs specific to Bass [fig. 12]. The presence of one such lantern above the stair adjacent to the nave and the appearance of a characteristic railing detail mark a point of overlap at which Bass's presence below is first asserted in Sterling.

Figure 13. View toward the Bass Library's study lounge and tile frieze from the landing of the tunnel from Sterling Memorial Library. *Timothy Hursley*.

Figure 14. Design for the repeating decorative panel in the tile frieze at the foot of the tunnel and stairway that joins Bass and Sterling. *Aric Lasher/HBRA*.

Within the interior, modern lighting fixtures with more sophisticated illumination characteristics are used in such a manner as to advance the conceit of Bass as an existing cellar that has been renovated for modern use. The louvered pendant fixtures used in the café and circulation areas are regarded as among the more iconic examples of twentieth-century lighting design and are variations of those first introduced in the 1920s by a Danish pioneer of modern illumination: designer, author, and social critic Poul Henningsen. These fixtures provide a glare-free light well suited to environments in which computers are used and have been in continuous production for more than half a century. This relationship of fixtures and furnishings, in which some are allied with the core architectural elements of the building while others demonstrate the introduction of more contemporary elements, characterizes the principles defining the broader strategy employed for the furnishings program of the library.

The decorative tile frieze at the foot of the tunnel and stairway that join Bass and Sterling declares a decisive moment of arrival at the new library. After passing between the gateposts and masonry piers of the stairwell and descending to the landing, a visitor is presented with an opaque recollection of the leaded upper windows of the Sterling nave [fig. 13]. Ceramic tile was chosen for this application as it shares material and modular attributes with Bass's architectural components of brick, stone, and glass. Tile possesses versatility as a repetitive unit that can also incorporate methods of handcraft and achieve a rich and var-

Figure 15. Design drawing for the wall-hung textiles in the group study rooms. The textiles were woven by Tibetan artisans for Odegard, Inc. *Aric Lasher/HBRA*.

ied quality of finish. The frieze's design applies the patterns and scale of leaded glazing found throughout Sterling and the metrical silhouette of the stair grille, gates, and glazed screens of the new library to evoke the effect of a backlit screen [fig. 14]. The source for the tile was an artisanal works whose founders have elaborated upon the methods and glazing techniques pioneered at the historic Pewabic Pottery, founded in the early twentieth century and acknowledged to be one of the preeminent arts and crafts tile works in North America. Molds for the tile were made from hand-drawn patterns provided by the architect, and hand-applied, proprietary glazes were selected for their luminosity and compatibility with the overall materials palette of the library. The variations that result from hand-molding and the irregularity of glazing mitigate the regularity of the pattern and enliven the surface. The repeating motif is broken at the center panel, where open book and motto, visible upon entering the tunnel from the lower level of Sterling, were incorporated as an appropriate herald of Bass's presence and purpose through use of Yale iconography.

Wall-hung textiles, which can be seen through the glazed upper walls of two-story spaces at the north and south sides of the building, serve an acoustic function but also establish a visual relationship between the library's upper and lower levels. Their design reinforces an overall ornamental program that takes the Cross Campus environment as its point of departure [fig. 15]. The linear pattern of the wall-hung rugs reiterates the vertical divisions of the metal screens and leaded upper panes of the library's glazed partitions, and the abstracted bud-blossom found at the center of each lancet is derived from the forged metal window guards at the Wall Street side of Sterling. The grilles' central motif is formed by the cleaving and bending of a central metal picket and is framed within the pointed arch of the window opening. The hangings' gradation of hue from blue to russet suggests a descent from sky to earth, and the rugs can be viewed from within the lower-level study rooms and collections areas as well as from adjacent spaces above. These panels were woven by Tibetan artisans in Nepal using native materials and techniques, along with yarns dyed by hand with extracts of local plants and blossoms. These were sourced by Odegard, a company whose social mission, funded by a portion of profits from sales, includes preservation of culturally valuable artisanal legacies as well as economic development within communities in which they are produced.

Furnishings for the library followed a clear and reasoned process of design and selection to support the overall architectural logic of the building while providing for the varied functional requirements of a contemporary facility with a nontraditional program. Infrastructural furnishings specifically speak to the fundamental architectural framework of masonry piers and paneled walls, while other elements accommodate more modern functional requirements as renovation furnishings. The twofold nature of furnishings and fixtures assembled for the library provided opportunities to address multiple architectural narratives while serving the often oppositional needs of program elements that ranged from study lounges and café to consulting areas, group study rooms, and technology-rich instructional areas.

Infrastructural furnishings include both custom-designed elements and those acquired from other sources. Components that reiterate the architectural program of the building include oak chairs, tables, carrels, computer stations, and teaching podia, as well as occasional tables found in lounge areas. Oak library seating takes as precedent chairs designed during the arts and crafts movement. Characterized by a chaste formal vocabulary and the integration of handicraft and artisanal embellishment, the arts and crafts movement produced various formal offspring, one of which was the American Collegiate Gothic style. Bass's chairs derive their form and method of assembly from designs by Gustav Stickley, C. R. Ashbee, and Greene Brothers, but they are closely related in material and design to the more robust and historically derived examples provided as part of the original furnishings program for the Sterling Library. These chairs were designed to complement Bass's more prosaic aesthetic, and the vertical silhouette of their slatted backs restates a motif present throughout the building. Reading tables, computer stations, and carrels share details and profiles with doors and wall panels, but their darker and smoother finish clearly sets them apart as furniture. These elements display common leg details, and their edge profiles are derived from sill and cap designs used for the library's stone components. Power, data connections, and lighting have been fully integrated, and custom-designed, data-enabled reading lamps on larger tables provide a mid-range of lighting and detail that is extended through the use of similar lamps at the paneled ends of book stacks.

Cast-iron tables found in café and lounge areas echo Bass's architectural elements in detail and material. These weighty pieces were conceived as relatively fixed islands around which moveable furnishings could be gathered. They were designed with the understanding that they would serve as foot rests as much as tables, and their heft and the profiled edges of their stone tops prevent damage and undesired movement. Their cast-iron frames, like the applied ornaments of the window system, were fabricated in sections, bolted together, and topped with slabs of alpine quartz, a more refined cousin of the green Burlington stone used for floors and countertops. Dimensions and proportions are those of designer Florence Knoll's classic modern tables, but their specific design reiterates that of the building's architecture. Moveable sign standards found throughout the library combine the tables' details with components found on handrails and grilles and serve as transitional elements between furnishings and architecture.

Lounge seating was also designed and chosen to reinforce an overall design narrative. Selected areas near entrances have been provided with chairs and settees designed in the 1920s by a figure of singular stature in the field of modern furniture design, architect Kaare Klint. These elements were seen as distinctly modern when introduced, but they derive their silhouettes and use of materials from Danish and English precedents. As such, they provide a transition between historically allusive seating found in Sterling and other more abstract items chosen for Bass. Wingback chairs are variations on another Danish design roughly based on eighteenth-century English prototypes. Characteristic upholstered lounge chairs chosen for Bass are of a more abstracted, style-indeterminate range that works well in both traditional and modern environments, and they were originally designed in the early twentieth century by Ludwig Mies van der Rohe for two of his early villa projects. Their character and materials are humble and durable, and their use extends the clublike atmosphere of such rooms as Sterling's Linonia and Brothers into the more informal open study areas of Bass. The design of these seating elements is stylistically transitional, and as such it mediates between the infrastructural and renovation palettes of furnishings found at Bass.

Furnishings to fulfill the functional needs of classroom environments and technology-rich settings were evaluated with regard to their compatibility with the renovation program. Iconic examples of modern American industrial design were chosen, including seating and tables designed by Charles and Ray Eames and sculptor Harry Bertoia. Eames, Bertoia, and Eero Saarinen, who designed the tables in the library café, studied and worked together under Saarinen's father at the Cranbrook Academy of Art, an institution whose foundation lay in the ethos of the arts and crafts movement and whose graduates successfully married modern methods and materials of industrial production with the principles of craft to produce the most significant and enduring body of work to be identified with American modernism. These industrially produced elements are easily distinguished from their handcrafted neighbors, but their status among the most important products of twentieth-century design and their qualitative excellence support the overall agenda of the furnishings palette. These items occupy the far end of a spectrum of furnishings that originates in the design of the early twentieth century. They have been integrated into the general realm of the Bass palette through use of characteristic upholstery materials and custom-designed table tops that share details and materials with more traditional items designed for the library. In a more abstract manner, the open silhouette of Bertoia's steel-gridded side chairs recalls that of the library's metallic components and as such finds a place in the courtyards and café.

Like the building's hybridized architectural expression, this intervening realm of transitional elements positions Bass within the larger ensemble of Cross Campus and the Sterling Memorial Library, allowing it to be at once familiar and distinct from its neighbors. The implementation of an overall program of furnishings and decorative arts served to catalyze the relationship between these earlier buildings and their subterranean extension and reinforced the architectural narrative of Bass as the renovated catacomb beneath Sterling and the Cross Campus green.

As a persuasive ensemble through which Yale's epic is literalized, revised, and displayed, the campus possesses far greater depth and meaning than any unconsidered collection of individual buildings, however notable. Expanding the library in a way that honored this notion demanded satisfaction of more than a hermetic set of architectural or programmatic objectives. Bass's innovative program extends the utility and hence the relevance of Sterling, and the new library's conceptual identity as undercroft derives purpose and legitimacy from a reciprocal relationship with its context. Bass is a modern building that reintroduces a middle ground of embellishment and material eloquence characteristic of Yale's architecture to impart meaning and engage its patrons and its surroundings. A legible building grounded in its time and place, the library strives to participate in the discourse of the Yale campus. Through strategic approaches to organization and architectural expression, the design seeks to address the current needs of the university library within a broader historical and institutional narrative. As with Cross Campus Library and all Yale buildings, Bass's longevity will ultimately be determined by its ability to inspire affection and convincingly fulfill this role amid changing circumstances and over time.

NOTES

1. See Patrick L. Pinnell, *The Campus Guide: Yale University* (Princeton, NJ: Princeton University Press, 1999), 78–79. Goodhue was the architect of notable landmarks such as St. Bartholomew's Church in New York City, the Rockefeller Chapel at the University of Chicago, the Los Angeles Public Library, and the Nebraska State Capitol. His work is distinguished by an exuberant and often abstracting application of historically derived motifs. Rogers's work encompassed residential and institutional buildings and was varied in its expression. His early work in Chicago was allied with that of other practitioners of its emerging commercial idiom, and his later design for the expansion of Yale's campus exploited modern construction methods and an eclectic, scenographic application of historical styles.

2. Ibid., 81–82.

3. Kent Bloomer, *The Nature of Ornament* (New York: W. W. Norton, 2000), 178.

4. Ibid., 184.

5. Ibid.

6. Skidmore, Owings and Merrill (SOM) was the most notable disseminator of the so-called American Corporate style, and the firm's adaptation of the tenets of European modernism to a variety of building types produced iconic examples of remarkable quality. SOM was a large organization that sought to suppress individual authorship, but the work of specific partners within the firm stands out and is typically associated with them. Its oeuvre from this "heroic" period includes Washington, D.C.'s Hirschorn Museum, the United States Air Force Academy, Chicago's John Hancock Center, and Lever House in New York.

7. Saarinen's brief career produced a remarkable if heterogeneous body of work characterized by a bold and formally expressive expansion of the boundaries of orthodox modernism. The son of a revered pioneer of Finnish architecture, Saarinen is perhaps best known for his terminals at Dulles and Kennedy airports, the Gateway Arch in St. Louis, and his designs for furnishings for the Knoll furniture company. His Yale buildings include Yale's David S. Ingalls Rink and Morse and Ezra Stiles Colleges.

8. Mies van der Rohe's work, most broadly identified with the refinement of an architectural language that would become the model for the glass-box modernism of the international style, demonstrates an overarching classicizing tendency. This is evident in its development and application of a hierarchical, classicized "order" of nonhistorical architectural elements and rules for their combination, as well as its frequent exploitation of symmetrical plan organization as a legible, rational, and "perfect" means of reconciling complex and contradictory programmatic demands.

DANUTA A. NITECKI

Rethinking Library Spaces

Libraries are environments that foster and support relationships among collections of information, researchers, and the teaching, learning, and research activities that transform information into knowledge. Traditionally, libraries at Yale University have developed around collections, mostly of books, supported by quiet spaces for reading and study. In the early 1970s a new type of library, the Cross Campus Library, was introduced to give primacy to study and access to a core collection of print resources. Designed by Edward Larrabee Barnes, Cross Campus Library (better known as CCL) was an underground, two-story facility with enclosed individual reading rooms, open spaces with tables for students to work together or alone, an assortment of comfortable seating, and, added over time, a few classrooms and an instruction room equipped with computers. Operating hours were longer than at other campus libraries, and over the years CCL became a popular student hangout and social space. After nearly thirty years of heavy use and natural deterioration, however, the facility's infrastructure needed to be upgraded and repaired. This offered an opportunity to rethink the library's physical space while also addressing changes in information technologies, teaching practices, and learning activities that had taken place since the library was first conceived and opened. The renovation of Cross Campus Library in 2006–07 by the architectural firm Hammond Beeby Rupert Ainge transformed this central campus library space into the Anne T. and Robert M. Bass Library, which opened to a crowd of over one thousand students, faculty, and staff at midnight on October 19, 2007.

The planning and design process behind this transformation initiated new ways of thinking about the relationships of bricks and bites and about the changing role of the library in its relationship to readers and information in the digital age. This essay explores two broad topics that defined the library's response to changes both in the academic community and in the nature of information: the evolution of the library from collector and accumulator to facilitator of collaboration between different partners, and the spatial characteristics that bridge and facilitate this evolution.

THE LIBRARY'S EMERGING ROLE

For centuries the most recognized role of the library has been that of the *accumulator* of books. Libraries are institutions that purposefully collect publications and artifacts of human communication, endeavor, and creativity. They preserve them and give them context through cataloged organization and curated access. Librarians, those who carry out this role and act as stewards, are titled after the buildings that house these collections.

In this model librarians use knowledge of scholarship and bibliographic

Bass Library Pavilion. *Michael Marlsand, Yale University.*

tools within a clearly defined scope to meet an institutional mission. They respond to user requests by describing the organizational structure of collections. Space is required to house collections and to provide quiet areas where they can be used. Interaction with the library can be minimal, limited to what is needed to navigate the collection, but it can also be overwhelming when it involves the use of complicated tools like catalogs, subject headings, and classification schemes. Sterling Memorial Library, which opened in 1930, is an example of the library as accumulator with its massive and imposing stack tower, handsome card catalog room, and large reading rooms.

Building on the roles of collector and steward, librarians have also acted as *information consultants*. Combining bibliographic expertise with interviewing skills, librarians interpret needs and provide guidance in locating and accessing information. They design customized search strategies and online system interfaces. In this model, greater value is placed on access to information than on ownership. Teaching the skills needed to locate and evaluate information sources is fundamental, and delivery and access networks, like circulation, reserve, interlibrary loan systems, and licensed electronic resources, are critical to success. Access to materials is made convenient, fast, and effortless, and the library user is seen as a consumer of library goods and services. In this way the library begins to respond to changes in user behavior in the digital age. As a center for consultation, libraries aim to address expectations of quality that include the user's own self-sufficiency, ease, and ability to find needed information and access to resources anytime and from anywhere.

The evolution of information technologies and changes in the nature of communication have created natural opportunities for the library to assume a new leadership role in *creating knowledge*. Now, librarians draw upon their bibliographic and consultative expertise in order to build partnerships with students, faculty, and other colleagues throughout the academy, maximizing the institution's ability to create and share knowledge. The library and its users coexist less as servant and consumers and more as partners or participants in production of information. The library as place is less a house of collections or a service point, and more a space where information seeking, learning, teaching, and research define the library.

THE LIBRARY AS LEARNING COMMONS

The library's evolving role in accumulation, providing access, and collaborating with new partners, including faculty and technology specialists, requires new and ongoing ways of thinking about its physical spaces. Scott Bennett, Yale University Librarian Emeritus, observes from his research on library construction that "the weight of traditional thinking about libraries . . . keeps planning focused not on the educational impact but on the service operations of libraries. Traditionally, library buildings are places where we shelve material, circulate things to readers, assist readers with questions about information resources, create instruments such as the catalog for navigating information, and teach readers how to master the complexities of both printed and networked information."[1]

As the role of the library changes, the design of the library as a place calls for new spaces to facilitate reflection, quick and easy assess to information, conversation, collaboration, and knowledge creation.

Several forces have created opportunities to renovate or build new libraries in support of their new roles. Historically, the major force for library expansion was an existing library's overcrowdedness, coupled with heavy use or deteriorating facilities. Space is both the most permanent and the scarcest resource on a university campus, and the maintenance of physical plants is becoming increasingly more difficult. Nearly $4.5 billion was spent on academic library space renovation or new construction in the United States during the 1990s, with additional operating budget costs of $90.5 million by 2001.[2] Library buildings are aging, and large research libraries like Yale's Sterling Memorial Library, Harvard's Widener Library, and Columbia's Butler Library, among others, were built during the early- to mid-twentieth century and have either had or now require major renovations. Even buildings completed during the second half of the twentieth century, like the Beinecke and newly renovated Art and Architecture Libraries at Yale, have required significant upgrades. Common demands are waterproofing, upgrading mechanical systems, increasing infrastructure for data and electricity, as well as accommodating persons with disabilities and other challenges in physical circulation, solutions for which often can be achieved only through major renovations. Such projects may require gutting and rebuilding interior spaces, offering opportunity to plan how a library might change both its layout and its programs of instruction, access, and learning.

Twenty-five years ago, transfer of less frequently consulted materials to high-density, off-site shelving facilities was introduced to address overcrowded stacks and shelves. Yale partially adopted this solution by building the Seeley G. Mudd Library in the early 1980s. While Mudd was envisioned as a repository for low-use materials, it was located on the central Yale campus and was accessible to users. Almost two decades later, the Library Shelving Facility, designed by Bruce Scott, opened in November 1998; by 2009, it housed more than three million items. The facility features modern environmental controls to ensure long-term preservation and is linked to a reliable daily delivery of materials to the central campus. Together, this arrangement supports the accumulator and access roles of the library while freeing up much-needed space in libraries across the Yale system for consulting and other user-based activities.

The demands of library users are also changing. Fundamental changes in the way students learn have resulted in increased engagement with coursework, as teachers incorporate problem-solving materials and experiential learning in their assignments. Some libraries are beginning to support these changes by reconfiguring existing spaces to create student lounges to facilitate group study and social learning. Increased availability of digital information is another factor influencing library spaces. Libraries have incorporated new technologies in their spaces since the 1960s, but the introduction of computers and the World Wide Web has been one of the most important events and influences in the history of libraries and information management. Over the past fifteen years new space requirements have emerged to accommodate fast network access, high-quality printing, word processing, photocopying, scanning, and online communication.

The 1990s also witnessed the emergence of the "library as place" movement. The library expanded its function to support both social activities and student learning outside the classroom by introducing coffee shops or cafés, revising food and drink policies, extending hours, providing Internet access, and creating comfortable and inviting spaces for academic work. The notion of the library as a silent space designed for only individual study was slowly revised if not abandoned.

During a 2005 conference sponsored by EDUCAUSE, a nonprofit association that promotes the intelligent use of information technology in education, discussion of the return to human-centered design of informal learning spaces led to comparisons between the "Information Commons" and the "Learning Commons."[3] The Information Commons introduced banks of computer workstations where students worked alone and in silence with limited support from librarians or information technologists. In contrast, the Learning Commons emphasizes social learning where faculty join students in communal spaces to create information in a social environment where silence is not the rule and, to a degree, food and drink are encouraged, or at least tolerated. Six years prior to this conference, librarians, through observing student behaviors and in conversation with faculty and planners at Yale, conceived the renovated Cross Campus Library as a Learning Commons equipped with teaching technologies and various environments to meet needs for individual study, group discussion and problem solving, classroom teaching, and delivery of assistance from campus experts in information resources, instructional technologies, and innovative pedagogy. These plans for transforming the role of the library were articulated conceptually in a report in 1999 before the ideas of social learning principles and the Information Commons were mainstreamed, or at least widely familiar on campus.[4]

THE ANNE T. AND ROBERT M. BASS LIBRARY

The renovated Bass Library illustrates the two themes discussed in this essay: the evolving roles of the library, and the spatial characteristics that define and support these new roles.

A core collection of basic and high-use materials defined Cross Campus Library when it opened. Some observed that it provided students with an alternative to Sterling Memorial Library, with the assumption that CCL was the "undergraduate" study library as distinguished from the more serious research library above ground. The building was designed to house a collection of approximately 150,000 books, but it grew to nearly 250,000 items reflecting all of the subjects taught at Yale. The library also featured small enclosed study spaces affectionately called "Weenie Bins," pinwheel clusters of individual study carrels, tables for four readers, and a number of brightly colored and movable vinyl block-like seats and sofas. Natural light was limited, the modern, minimal furnishings and all-white decor quickly became worn, and the eventual installation of computers and other hardware proved difficult and unsightly. Over time, occupants facilitated social activity by moving furniture, cramming groups of two and sometimes more students into a Weenie Bin, or gathering at tables to create a congenial atmosphere during late-night hours. The observed study practices of social interactions, ownership and redefining of space, consumption of food and drink, and the escalation of noise in the library led planners to conceive of a new concept of a library and designers to visualize new spaces. The Learning Commons emerged as a metaphor for a renovated library, emphasizing shared space, collaborative learning, and integrated access to both print and online information.

Based on these observations, construction project documents for the Bass Library included resources like forty-four individual study rooms, an informal study café, eight two-story group-study rooms around the two sides of the building to suggest natural light and soaring openness, a variety of carrels and leather chairs around the naturally lit courtyards, and 15,000 linear feet of shelving to house a reconstituted collection of 150,000 items of various formats. Experimentation in ways to converge technologies, pedagogy, and information content to support teaching and learning continues in two flexibly defined classrooms and through a variety of programs and individual consultations involving faculty, librarians, and other expert groups on campus. The Collaborative Learning Center, located on the lower level of the library, draws faculty, students, and staff for customized and routine technology assistance. Lively discussions also occur in the Thain Family Café or in any of the fourteen group study rooms. Wireless access to the Internet and online resources is available throughout the library. Furniture is movable, and its spatial arrangements are redefined daily by library users. The library has once again become an energetic and stimulating place, experienced in an open and engaging environment.

REMAINING QUESTIONS TO EXPLORE

The evaluation of the library's contribution to educational outputs and outcomes remains a challenge. Changes and continual assessment of the evolving role of the library are among two of the most important issues addressed when rethinking the library as a place. Librarians at Yale have been fortunate to have opportunities in recent years to do so. In collaboration with campus partners, we have reflected on how the academic experience is changing, what services are helpful to enable such innovations, and how to design spaces that facilitate and support teaching, learning, and research. A few questions for further research and discussion may illustrate the ongoing nature of rethinking the role and appearance of the library.

What future changes in library spaces, both at Yale and beyond, will be required as more information is available digitally? Are we using these spaces effectively? Earlier we felt an obligation to provide computers in adequate numbers to ensure access to electronic texts and databases. Are we facing different demands as information is increasingly visual and includes audio and/or online components? Does the library's role of facilitating access remain constant, which in turn creates changing expectations about the type of equipment that should be available in the library?

Are aesthetic details cost-effective investments? What contribution does attention to the environment's design and decoration put on access to information or its use? As we think about engagement with information as an element of learning, we discover the importance of social learning, and with that come new questions about the attractiveness of space as a stimulus to social discourse. How important are food or drink, comfortable seating, and flexible movement of furniture for bringing people together or encouraging collaboration?

Finally, what is the impact of renovated library spaces? Longitudinal information on the outcomes of information commons and learning spaces is just becoming available and invites future research. At Yale, a grant-supported project examined the impact on teaching of using digital images and developed rubrics to suggest how to gauge different levels of teaching and learning with this resource.[5] During this exploration, faculty repeatedly expressed their frustrations with facilities for both teaching and course preparations. This insight informed design decisions in creating the Bass Library as a Learning Commons, as well as the Collaborative Learning Center within it as a virtual and physical environment for exploration.

These are just a few of the questions that face libraries and that may benefit from further research and shared dialogue. In the meantime, the Bass Library is now recognized as a transformative place at Yale where students, faculty, librarians, and other experts come together to transform information into knowledge.

NOTES

1. Scott Bennett, *Libraries Designed for Learning* (Washington, DC: Council on Library and Information Resources, 2003), 5.

2. Ibid., 6–7.

3. For further discussion, see Joan K. Lippincott, "Linking the Information Commons to Learning," *Learning Spaces,* ed. Diana G. Oblinger. Available at http://www.educause.edu/learningspacesch7.

4. Scott Bennett and Danuta A. Nitecki, "The Library as Learning Space," in *Report of the Planning Committee for Phase 2a Library Renovation* (Attachment 5) (New Haven, CT: Yale University Library, 1999). Available at http://www.library.yale.edu/renovaxn/phase2a/P2A%20Archive.html.

5. Danuta A. Nitecki and William Rando, "Evolving an Assessment of the Impact on Pedagogy, Learning and Library Support of Teaching with Digital Images," in *Outcomes Assessment in Higher Education Views and Perspectives,* ed. Peter Hernon and Robert E. Dugan (Englewood, CO: Libraries Unlimited, 2004), 175–96.

LAURA TATUM

The Architectural Archives at Yale University Library

Yale University has long recognized the value of retaining drawings, maps, deeds, correspondence, and other documentation of its architectural and real estate holdings. Architectural records are invaluable to the University in case of legal disputes, as documentation of earlier work when a building renovation is undertaken, and as evidence of the architect's design intent. As research tools, architectural records are used by architectural historians; students of architecture, urban studies, and material culture; practicing architects; and community members seeking to understand the landscape they inhabit. Architectural drawings are also often valuable for exhibition purposes.

For decades, archivists in the Department of Manuscripts and Archives in the Yale University Library have sought to comprehensively collect and make available the architectural records of the University. More recently, Manuscripts and Archives has undertaken an active collecting program for drawings, correspondence, photographs, and other documentation of the work designed by prominent graduates of the Yale School of Architecture, as well as by local architecture firms that have made a significant contribution to the built environment of New Haven and surrounding areas. This essay describes collecting strategies, beginning with early attempts to identify and consolidate all architectural drawings located within and related to the University; cataloging and making available surrogates of each drawing on microfilm "aperture cards"; collaboration among various departments and schools within the University to encourage the formation of a cohesive architectural archives program; and, finally, Manuscripts and Archives' current endeavor to collect the work of large, active, contemporary architects and architectural firms with close ties to Yale and New Haven.

Some of the earliest architectural records at Yale are found in manuscript collections that, at first glance, would not seem to hold much promise for architectural historians. Collections such as the Hillhouse Family Papers, the John Ferguson Weir Papers, and the Fabrique Family Papers contain such treasures as plat maps of early New Haven; drawings from some of the best-known residential architects of the day, including Alexander Jackson Davis, architect of the Hillhouse family residence that stood on the site of the present Kline Biology Tower; sketchbooks documenting travels on a Grand Tour of Europe; and, in the case of the Fabrique Family Papers, some of the earliest drawings of vernacular residential architecture in Connecticut. Manuscripts and Archives also holds early drawings of the New Haven Green, with the three churches as its centerpiece, as well as of the old campus—well before its current incarnation as the "Old Campus." Known as the "Bowen Plan" and the "Doolittle engraving," these drawings are housed in Record Unit (RU) 703, Yale University Buildings and Grounds Photographs. These early drawings hold a great deal of fascination for undergraduates and researchers with Yale or New Haven ties, as the changes in the campus—and in strategies for campus planning—manifest themselves in these hand-drawn materials.

In the late 1970s, Lawrence Dowler, then Director of Manuscripts and Archives, became acutely concerned about the state of the existing architectural documentation at Yale. Most of the drawings for campus buildings were spread out in various buildings and departments, but particularly in the Plan Room of the University's Architectural and Engineering Services Department (now the Office of Facilities). There was no central repository designated for the materials, nor any single access point for researchers. Moreover, a large number of these drawings were housed in less than ideal conditions, primarily hanging from racks in engineering storage cabinets, with anywhere from fifty to one hundred drawings on each rack. This contributed to the accelerated disintegration of drawings on unstable media, such as blueprints on acidic paper, which were often the only extant documentation of campus buildings. Original drawings, among them ink-on-trace detail drawings by James Gamble Rogers for his campus buildings, were found folded in boxes without any sort of inventory, making it impossible for researchers to identify individual projects and request those drawings.

Enraged and emboldened, Dowler applied for and received a $50,000, eighteen-month grant from the National Endowment for the Humanities in 1977 to create a centralized repository for the University's architectural drawings. The project had many goals: survey the University and collect architectural drawings from various repositories; create an inventory of all of these drawings in order to make them accessible to researchers; update the *Buildings and Grounds of Yale University* pamphlet, last published in 1965, to include references to extant drawings in Manuscripts and Archives' holdings; identify those drawings in need of conservation treatment and, working with the Library's Conservation Studio, conserve them according to best practices; and, finally, microfilm each of the drawings to ensure that the information on even the most fragile of the drawings would be preserved.

One set of this microfilm would be cut into individual frames with each frame representing one drawing or, in the case of extremely large drawings, one section of a drawing, and mounted onto aperture cards. An aperture card is a computer-readable punch card with a piece of microfilm mounted onto it. The idea behind the aperture card project was manifold. First, each piece of microfilm corresponding to (in most cases) one individual drawing would be physically readable by a researcher. Second, it would be identifiable by a seventeen-category system of encoding that would allow the researcher to identify not only the building the drawing pertained to, but also the date of the drawing, the part of the building shown, and the date the building became a Yale property. Third, the encoded punch card would enable Manuscripts and Archives to create, when

"A View of the Buildings of Yale College at New Haven" by A. B. Doolittle, 1807.
Yale University Buildings and Grounds Photographs (RU 703).
Manuscripts and Archives, Yale University Library.

funding for the technology was available, a computerized database of all of the individual drawings in the repository.

Tawny Ryan Nelb, an archivist specializing in architectural materials, was hired as project manager for this ambitious endeavor. Her first step was to ask individual departments to send any architectural drawings that they held to Manuscripts and Archives. While most departments were glad to be rid of these large, unwieldy, fragile materials, the Plan Room was more reluctant to relinquish its holdings. Here, the eternal debate about the intended use of architectural drawings reared its head. Are the drawings generated by architects in the course of erecting and renovating physical buildings *technical tools* in perpetual use by engineers and archivists? Or, once a building has been completed, are they important *archival documentation* to be used by researchers and scholars? Are the most beautiful drawings, such as presentation drawings—made to seduce clients with a renderer's fantastic impression of a building—actually art objects, to be savored by art historians and occasionally exhibited in museums or galleries? Without fully resolving the controversy, a compromise was reached: original drawings for which blueprints existed would be sent to Manuscripts and Archives, while blueprints or other reproduced prints would remain in the Plan Room. Original drawings for which there were no surrogates would also remain in the Plan Room until funding could be secured for reproduction. The Architectural and Engineering Services Department also agreed to insert a clause into contracts

Entrance to Henry Austin's New Haven Cemetery, more commonly known as
the Grove Street Cemetery, 1848.
Henry Austin Papers (MS 1084). Manuscripts and Archives.

for all University buildings requiring the commissioned architect to deposit one set of as-built and presentation drawings with Manuscripts and Archives. To date, however, this stipulation has been followed rarely, if at all.

Despite this compromise, the number of drawings that Manuscripts and Archives originally anticipated finding in other University departments exceeded all initial estimates. The initial proposal called for approximately 6,500 drawings in Manuscripts and Archives to be filmed, re-housed, and catalogued, along with approximately 1,500 from elsewhere in the University. By the time the project (which extended well beyond the grant funding period) was finished, over thirteen thousand drawings had been filmed, catalogued, and re-housed, with over eight hundred having been treated in the Library's Conservation Studio. To make the record as complete as possible, additional drawings for University projects were borrowed for microfilming from local repositories such as the New Haven Building Department and the New Haven Colony Historical Society.

The James Gamble Rogers Papers alone contributed nearly two thousand additional fragile, folded, and enormous full-scale detail drawings to the project, many measuring twenty-four square feet in size. The Library's Conservation Studio undertook all conservation treatment and encapsulation of drawings in-house, including these large Rogers drawings. Many drawings of University buildings had been mounted on board with cheap adhesive, which had to be painstakingly scraped from its acidic backing. Another major problem with architectural drawings, both then and now, is the tendency for architects to repair any tears with Scotch tape. A conservator's nightmare, Scotch tape either tends to dry out and fall off, leaving an acidic, brittle yellow residue in its wake, or the adhesive disintegrates into a viscous ooze, sticking to itself and other drawings surrounding it. The staff in the Conservation Studio valiantly tackled these and other issues of brittleness, media instability, and size in order to make the drawings secure enough for filming and re-housing. The James Gamble Rogers drawings, when their existence came to light as a result of this project, were of particular interest to curators at the Yale University Art Gallery. A large exhibition of these hand-drawn elevations, sections, and details was mounted in 1982, entitled "Sparing No Detail: The Drawings of James Gamble Rogers for Yale University, 1913–1935." Seventy-three of the exhibited works were borrowed from Manuscripts and Archives.

Cataloguing thirteen thousand individual drawings was no easy task, especially when the drawings were presented in no order whatsoever. Considering the number of University projects for which Manuscripts and Archives now held drawing documentation, Nelb and her assistants had no choice but to catalog material in batches, undifferentiated by project or date. They devised a seventeen-category system by which each drawing could be uniquely identified, both in an eye-readable inventory and on machine-readable aperture cards. They also devised two main categories, "region" and "chronology," in order to point to specific buildings, many of which had had a variety of names over the years. "Region" was based on a twenty-eight-square grid, created by the archivists, to delineate regions of the campus. For example, Region 1 described the Old Campus, bounded by Elm, Chapel, High, and College Streets. "Chronology" then indicated the order in which buildings were acquired by the University within each region. Other descriptive categories included date, architect, drawing type, drawing size, drawing medium, and several others to help identify individual frames of microfilm. This intensive cataloguing and coding was done so that any researcher could view any individual drawing without staff having to retrieve and transport entire folders. Nelb's progress notes from the period indicate that drawings by Henry Austin, Alexander Jackson Davis, and James Gamble Rogers were those most often requested by researchers.

In 1984 funding was secured to convert the data on the machine-readable aperture cards into a database of all architectural drawings in the department. The cards were to be read by what was then the Yale Computer Center and stored on magnetic tape to create a database. A printout of this database and all of the aperture cards remain available as a research resource in Manuscripts and Archives. This project was considered a pioneering tool for making architectural drawings more accessible to researchers; archivists and curators from repositories around the country, including the Massachusetts Institute of Technology and the

Avery Architectural and Fine Arts Library at Columbia University, came to study the project. Nelb also gave several public presentations about the project, including one at the 1982 annual meeting of the Society of Architectural Historians. The revised edition of *Buildings and Grounds of Yale University*, published in 1979, served as an informal guide to the drawings available in Manuscripts and Archives. A more formal finding aid to Record Unit 1 was also made available in the department, with Series I representing all materials filmed up to 1983, Series II representing all unfilmed drawings accessioned through 1985, and Series III representing all future accessions of material. This finding aid has recently undergone significant revision by Manuscripts and Archives staff.

Despite the conversion of the aperture cards into a database of individual drawings, accessibility remained a major stumbling block for researchers. In 1993 Val Woods, then Senior Architect/Planner in the Office of Facilities, wrote a memo to Manuscripts and Archives Director Richard Szary: "The only available index of building drawings at the present time is the Series I microfiche list developed by MSSA. . . . The microfiche coding . . . is rather difficult to fathom. Therefore it is hard to research a particular drawing since the code also does not contain a reference to drawing number or title."[1] Woods's concerns about accessibility—or lack thereof—were spurred on by a renewed interest in Yale's architectural records by faculty, most prominently George Hersey of the Department of the History of Art and John Cook of the Divinity School. Another 1993 memo from Woods to Hersey and his research assistant, Susan Ryan, asked several forward-thinking questions that would lead to great changes in Manuscripts and Archives' collecting focus over the next decade, and raised the question of whether a dedicated repository for architectural records would be appropriate: "Original drawings and design sketches: can consultant architects be persuaded to give their original drawings of Yale-commissioned buildings to MSSA? Can they be persuaded to give their whole drawing archives to Yale? Is MSSA prepared to accept more drawings? Does a new Architectural Archive make better sense?"[2]

Eager to accept the challenges implied in Woods's memo, Szary began talks with Millicent Abell, the University Librarian, regarding a possible grant to fund a pilot transfer of drawings amassed in the previous decade from the Plan Room to Manuscripts and Archives, and to "investigate the issues surrounding the preservation of appropriate documentation that only exists in CAD format."[3] CAD (computer-aided drafting) was, in 1993, a relatively new technology being adopted by architecture firms. The question of how best to preserve digital design data began then and is now a major issue for architectural archivists around the world. While Yale was certainly prescient in acknowledging the issues presented by CAD documentation in 1993, archivists in Manuscripts and Archives continue to struggle with real-life solutions to these storage and access problems today.

In the end, no formal grant project to transfer architectural drawings from one department to another took place, but in 1999 Szary and archivist Kirsten Jensen attempted to migrate the aperture card system to a more easily accessible

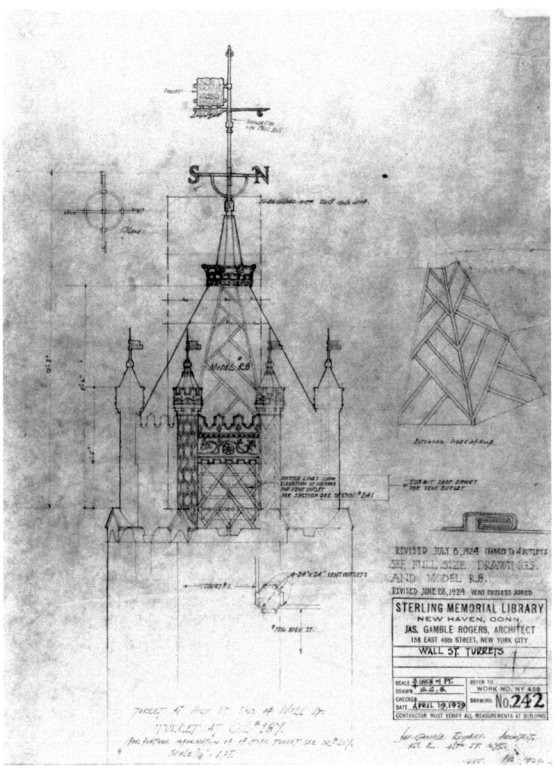

Design by James Gamble Rogers for a turret on Sterling Memorial Library at High and Wall Streets.
Sterling Memorial Library, Yale University, Photographs (RU 696). Manuscripts and Archives.

digital database of scanned images. A project was planned to scan all physical drawings in the department, as well as the thirty-four uncut reels of microfilm that were generated during the aperture card filming project. A number of potential vendors were contacted, but each ran up against a major stumbling block: file size. Architectural drawings are by nature very large, and creating eye-readable digital images requires a great deal of storage space. At the time, the Library's server capacities required that each scanned image be no larger than sixty-four megabytes. Unfortunately, this limit proved impossible to meet while still producing useful images of architectural drawings. The current best practice in Manuscripts and Archives is to send large-format drawings out of the department to be digitally photographed, rather than scanned, and only upon researcher request. This is better stewardship for the physical drawings and provides a high-quality digital image for the researcher. The average file size for these images is approximately four hundred megabytes.

The major catalyst for what would eventually become the Architectural Archives program (apart from the University buildings drawings, which are part of the University Archives, along with all documentation of the Yale School of Architecture) was a memo drafted by Richard Szary and Max Marmor, then the Director of the Arts Library, in 2000. Addressed to Dean Robert A.M. Stern of the School of Architecture and Thomas J. Crow, then the Chairman of the Department of the History of Art, the multipage memo describes the need for a systematic approach to collecting the complete design output of the most influential graduates of the Yale School of Architecture, or those who otherwise have significant

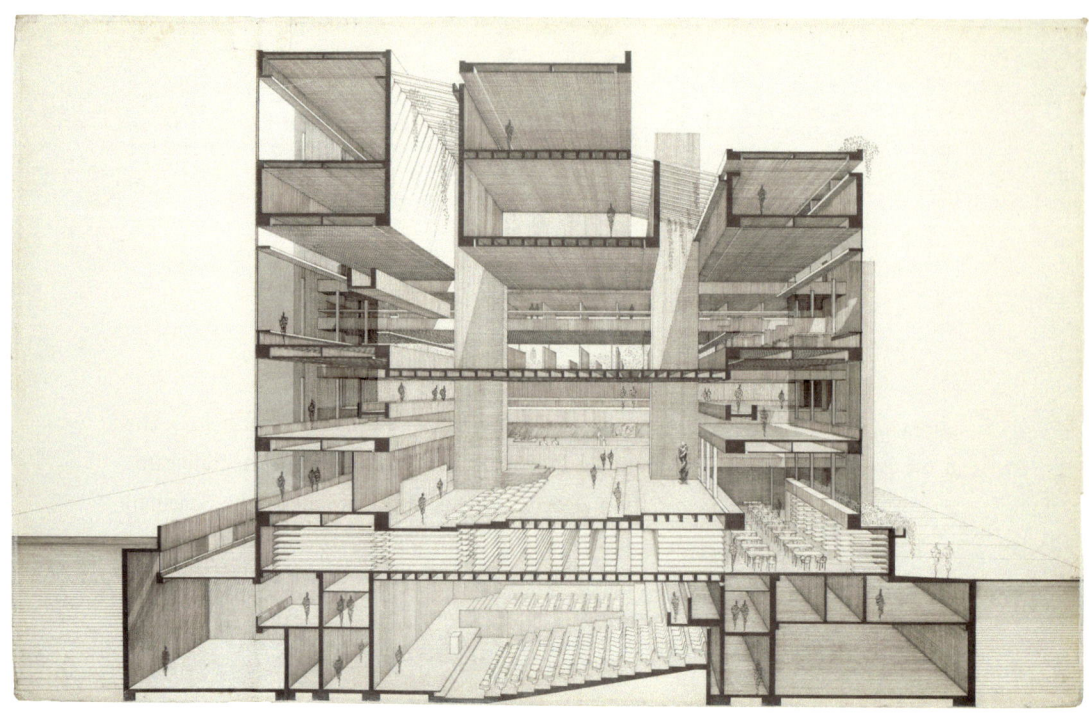

Perspective section of Paul Rudolph's design for the Art + Architecture Building, c. 1958.
School of Architecture, Yale University, Memorabilia (RU 925).
Manuscripts and Archives.

Yale connections: "In view of the singular role that Yale has played both in the field of architecture and in the scholarly study of the history of architecture, it is rather surprising that Yale has never had a sustained program in this area. Manuscripts and Archives does hold a number of architecture-related collections . . . but these holdings represent the serendipitous and opportunistic acquisition of such materials, rather than a focused program, and a number of them are limited segments of the individual's papers, rather than comprehensive collections."[4]

To take advantage of the Library's existing architectural records expertise, it was agreed that Manuscripts and Archives would be the appropriate home for this new program, the goals for which were outlined with a number of bullet points but boiled down to one major theme: this would be a collection developed for the purposes of teaching and research. Faculty would be encouraged to bring their art history and architecture students to Manuscripts and Archives to use the materials—not just to view them, but to open rolls of drawings, leaf through correspondence and photographs, and make use of the materials in projects and scholarship. Szary and Marmor emphasized that Manuscripts and Archives would be highly selective in the acquisition of collections, and that they expected most of the materials to be donated, not purchased. They recommended that a curator for the collection be hired, as well as sufficient staff to support the continuous processing and preservation efforts. Szary and Marmor also addressed the need for further research into the delivery of digital surrogates of the material, as well as preservation issues for born-digital design data.

Almost as soon as this memo was written and received, the Architectural Archives program was off and running. Stern and Szary immediately began to solicit donations from prominent alumni of the School of Architecture and also courted donors whose papers were already, in part, housed in Manuscripts and Archives. One of those very early donors was Kevin Roche, Principal of Kevin Roche John Dinkeloo Associates (KRJDA). KRJDA is the Pritzker Prize–winning successor firm to Eero Saarinen and Associates, Saarinen being one of the most influential mid-century American architects and, importantly, a Yale graduate. Saarinen's widow, Aline, had given a small collection of Saarinen's papers to Yale in 1971, but the majority of the architectural drawings, photographs, contracts, specifications, and other documentation were still held at the at the KRJDA office in Hamden, Connecticut, a short drive from the Yale campus. After a period of negotiation, Roche agreed to donate all of the Saarinen material to Yale. In 2004 the Getty Foundation funded two concurrent projects pertaining to the Saarinen collection: a fifteen-month processing grant for the collection materials themselves, and a research grant for a major monograph and international exhibition of the Saarinen collection to be coordinated among many institutions. The research portion of this project began in 2004, and the processing of the collection began in earnest when a project archivist was hired a year later.

The high-profile nature of the Saarinen collection served as a lightning rod for other architects eager to donate their papers. Many of the donors, including Cesar Pelli and Warren Platner, had a connection to Saarinen, while others had strong ties to Yale, among them Robert A.M. Stern Architects; Cooper, Robertson and Associates; and Centerbrook Architects and Planners. Manuscripts and Archives was eager to collect the records of these prominent alumni and associates, but the space and staffing limitations were daunting. The project archivist hired for the Saarinen project was not a permanent member of the Manuscripts and Archives staff, and the department's processing team and work area could not handle the voluminous output of these successful firms. The entire Saarinen collection is composed of 379 tubes of drawings and sixty-nine linear feet of associated documentation, representing Saarinen's brilliant but short career. By way of comparison, each accession of material from Robert A.M. Stern Architects, representing approximately a year of work, consists of approximately 150 tubes of drawings and boxes of associated material. It would be impossible for Manuscripts and Archives to keep up with this kind of never-ending tidal wave of material, especially as more and more firms began to inquire about placing their archives at Yale or about signing gift agreements planning for the eventual placement of their archives at Yale.

Faced with this dilemma, Manuscripts and Archives developed a solution called "pre-custodial intervention." This mutually beneficial practice allows firms to establish their own work flows and timelines for transfer of materials to Yale while simultaneously giving an intellectual and physical order to the materials.

Mayor Richard C. Lee studying an architectural model of New Haven, 1963.
Richard Charles Lee Papers (MS 318). Manuscripts and Archives.

This, in turn, allows Manuscripts and Archives to provide immediate access to the donor firm's materials. As a condition of the gift, donor firms now agree to rehouse, arrange, and describe their own materials, by either hiring an archivist or designating a staff member to perform these tasks. The architectural archivist in Manuscripts and Archives (who was made a permanent staff member in 2007) travels to the firm and, over the course of several visits, works with the firm to develop good arrangement and description practices that align with University standards and national best practices for architectural records. Once the drawings and other records are transferred to Yale, the architectural archivist converts the firm's finding aid into Yale's encoded archival description (EAD) format and creates a catalog record for the collection in Orbis, the Library's online catalog. Manuscripts and Archives staff accession the collection, making it instantly available for research use.

This method of working collaboratively with firms has proved very rewarding in the past few years, particularly as faculty interests have begun to coincide with architects' donations. One recent example is Kevin Roche's donation of his own firm's papers. Yale School of Architecture Professor Eeva-Liisa Pelkonen, having served as principal researcher on the Getty grant for the Saarinen exhibition and monograph, was intrigued by the possibility of continuing that thread of her research by investigating the KRJDA collection. After Saarinen's death, Roche and his partner, John Dinkeloo, carried out design and construction on all of Saarinen's unfinished projects and began new projects of their own. Pelkonen, fascinated by what she discovered about the realization of these Saarinen projects, many of which were documented only in a piecemeal way in the Saarinen collection, delved deeper into the KRJDA collection and found it to be just as revelatory about broader architectural, social, and political changes. Almost as quickly as Manuscripts and Archives receives records from KRJDA, Pelkonen and her students collaboratively begin to incorporate them into research for an upcoming symposium, monograph, and exhibition. This kind of immediate service to the research needs of faculty and students would be impossible without the process of pre-custodial intervention.

Looking ahead, Manuscripts and Archives hopes to continue its research into the immediate, pressing, and complex issues of preserving born-digital design data. This is not a problem that one institution alone can solve. The architectural archivist and electronic records archivists work closely with their colleagues at other major architectural repositories, including the Massachusetts Institute of Technology, Columbia University, the University of Pennsylvania, and Harvard University, to determine best practices and attempt to forge alliances with CAD software developers, vendors, and donor firms themselves. The department has already received a small number of architectural records in digital format, and the transition from analog to digital design creation is complete within architectural firms. Before these records are lost to obsolete formats and software, Manuscripts and Archives must devote extensive amounts of time and significant resources to planning for the eventuality of accessioning and providing access to these records.

Manuscripts and Archives is also planning to work with local architects of significance with ties to the Yale School of Architecture or who have important built work in the New Haven area. Many researchers come to the department looking for documentation of buildings by local architects of prominence in the late nineteenth and early twentieth centuries; most of this documentation has not survived. By engaging actively with the local architecture community, the department hopes to document the best of the local built environment for future generations of New Haven scholars.

NOTES

1. Woods to Szary, unpublished memorandum, September 2, 1993, Manuscripts and Archives, Yale University.

2. Woods to Hersey, unpublished memorandum, May 25, 1993, Manuscripts and Archives, Yale University.

3. Szary to Abell, unpublished memorandum, August 26, 1993, Manuscripts and Archives, Yale University.

4. Szary and Marmor to Stern and Crow, unpublished memorandum, February 21, 2000, Manuscripts and Archives, Yale University.

APPENDIX

The following is a list of architectural collections in Manuscripts and Archives (including those with significant architectural components). Online access to finding aids and other archival holdings is available via www.library.yale.edu/mssa/.

MANUSCRIPT GROUPS

Henry Austin Papers (MS 1034)

Balmori Associates Records (MS 1885)

Jonathan Barnett Papers (MS 1733)

Frederick Bland Collection of Sketches of the Art + Architecture Building by Paul Rudolph (MS 1933)

Brooks Family Papers (MS 1784)

Elizabeth Mills Brown Files on New Haven Architecture (MS 1946)

Centerbrook Architects and Planners Records (MS 1844)

Serge Chermayeff Papers (MS 1240)

John W. Cook Interviews with Architects (MS 1873)

H. Page Cross Papers (MS 776)

William Adams Delano Papers (MS 178)

George Dudley Papers (MS 1861)

Fabrique Family Papers (MS 201)

Hyman I. Feldman Papers (MS 1887)

James Wilder Green Papers (MS 1891)

Harold Washington Library Center Collection (MS 1493)

Hillhouse Family Papers (MS 282)

Norman Morrison Isham Papers (MS 1156)

Louis Isadore Kahn Collection (MS 1345)

Richard Kelly Papers (MS 1838)

Richard Charles Lee Papers (MS 318)

Edward Joseph Logue Papers (MS 959)

Carroll L. V. Meeks Collection (MS 706)

Anthony John Monk Collection on Paul Rudolph (MS 1928)

Robert Moses Papers (MS 360)

Henry Killam Murphy Papers (MS 231)

New Haven Redevelopment Agency Records (MS 1814)

Pelli Clarke Pelli Architects Records (MS 1939)

Warren Platner Records (MS 1874)

Rice Family Papers (MS 415)

Greville Rickard Papers (MS 1227)

Kevin Roche John Dinkeloo Associates Records (MS 1884)

James Gamble Rogers Papers (MS 396)

Harold Wickliffe Rose Papers (MS 1239)

Maurice Emil Henri Rotival Papers (MS 1380)

Paul Marvin Rudolph Papers (MS 1411)

Eero Saarinen Collection (MS 593)

Vincent Scully Papers (MS 1872)

George Dudley Seymour Papers (MS 442)

C. Ray Smith Papers (MS 1948)

Robert A.M. Stern Architects Records (MS 1859)

Shepherd Stevens Papers (MS 865)

Ithiel Town Papers (MS 499)

John Trumbull Papers (MS 506)

Christopher Tunnard Papers (MS 1070)

Howard Sayre Weaver Papers (MS 1259)

John Ferguson Weir Papers (MS 550)

King-Lui Wu Papers (MS 1842)

Emanuel Zeid Collection (MS 1391)

RECORD UNITS

(including School of Architecture records concerning public events and publications)

Architectural Drawings and Maps of Yale University Buildings and Grounds (RU 1)

Architectural Documentation for Yale Buildings and Grounds (RU 2)

Assignment Plans for Yale University Buildings (RU 4)

Central Project Records for Yale University Building Projects (RU 5)

Office Files of Douglas Orr, Architect, Concerning the Addition to the Yale University Art Gallery (RU 241)

Art, Architecture, and Art History Theses and Projects, Yale University, 1915–2007 (RU 259)

Records of *Perspecta*, 1952–2002 (RU 336)

Recordings of Lectures and Presentations at the Yale Art Gallery and Yale Center for British Art (RU 359)

Pictures of Sterling Divinity Quadrangle (RU 628)

Yale University Buildings and Grounds Photographs (RU 703)

Photographs of the Art + Architecture Building, Yale University, by Ezra Stoller (RU 869)

School of Architecture, Yale University, lectures and presentations (RU 880)

School of Architecture, Yale University, records concerning events and exhibitions, 1970–2008 (RU 886)

School of Architecture, Yale University, exhibit materials from "Architecture or Revolution: Charles Moore and Architecture at Yale in the 1960s," c. 1965–2002 (RU 906)

Reminiscences and Memorabilia of Yale University Architecture Students in the Classes of 1948 to 1958 (RU 961)

Reminiscences and Documentation of Yale University Architecture Students Collected by Robert A.M. Stern (RU 1001)

Yale Building Project Photographs, 1967–2006 (RU 1078)

Contributors

Charles Gwathmey (1938–2009) studied architecture at Yale and co-founded Gwathmey Siegel and Associates in 1968. A student of Paul Rudolph's, he was chosen to renovate the Art + Architecture Building, which reopened in 2008. Gwathmey was Davenport Visiting Professor (1983 and 1999) and Bishop Visiting Professor (1991) at Yale University, and Eliot Noyes Visiting Professor at Harvard University (1985). He also taught at Princeton, Columbia, Cooper Union, and the University of California, Los Angeles. In his memory, Ralph and Ricky Lauren have established the Charles Gwathmey Professorship in Practice at the Yale School of Architecture.

Aric Lasher is an Architect Principal at Hammond Beeby Rupert Ainge, first joining the firm in 1985. He served as Project Architect for the Bass Library and related renovation work at the Sterling Memorial Library. He is a graduate of Cornell University's College of Architecture, Art, and Planning and has a master of fine art degree from the University of Southern California's School of Cinematic Arts. In addition to his work in architecture, he has designed sets for several motion pictures, including *Minority Report* and *Pearl Harbor*. He is co-author of *Plans of Chicago*, a book that examines the origins and future direction of planning in Chicago from an urban historical perspective.

Danuta A. Nitecki has been Associate University Librarian at Yale University since 1996 and directs public services and the Library's research education program. She served as the Library Program Director for the transformation of the Cross Campus Library into the Bass Library, and also represented the Library during the renovation of the Sterling Memorial Library stack tower and reading rooms, construction and expansions of the Library Shelving Facility, and the Arts Library renovation. She has a doctorate in library and information science from the University of Maryland.

Margaret K. Powell has been Librarian of the Lewis Walpole Library since 2000. She holds a doctorate in eighteenth- and nineteenth-century English literature and a master's degree in library science from the University of North Carolina at Chapel Hill. She has taught or held library positions at North Carolina, the University of Hawaii, and, since 1987 (with a brief time away at the Watkinson Library at Trinity College), Yale.

Alice Prochaska has been Yale University Librarian since 2001; previously, she was Director of Special Collections at the British Library. She received her undergraduate degree and doctorate from Oxford and will return there in 2010 as Principal of Somerville College. Her recent presentations and publications focus on the stewardship of international historic collections and the philosophy and ethics surrounding the notion of cultural restitution.

Mark Simon has been a Partner at Centerbook Architects and Planners since 1978. He received a bachelor's degree from Brandeis University and a master's degree in architecture from Yale. He developed sculptural skills at Brandeis and, after graduation from Yale, worked as a cabinetmaker, developing a concern for architectural detail. In 1990 he was made a Fellow of the American Institute of Architects. His practice ranges from private houses to commercial, institutional, academic, and religious projects.

Robert A.M. Stern is Dean of the Yale School of Architecture and J. M. Hoppin Professor of Architecture. A practicing architect, teacher, and writer, he is the founder and Senior Partner of Robert A.M. Stern Architects and a Fellow of the American Institute of Architects. He is the author of several books on architecture and the development of New York City's architecture and urbanism. In 1986 he hosted *Pride of Place: Building the American Dream*, a documentary television series aired on PBS. He has a bachelor's degree from Columbia University and a master's degree in architecture from Yale.

Laura Tatum is Architectural Records Archivist in the Department of Manuscripts and Archives at Yale University Library. Previously, she was Project Archivist at the University of California, Berkeley's Environmental Design Archives, and in 2002 she was the Kress Fellow in Art Librarianship at Yale. She has a bachelor's degree in English from Columbia University and a master's degree in information science from the University of Michigan.

Marjorie G. Wynne (1917–2009) joined the staff of the Yale University Library's Rare Book Room in 1942. In 1963 she moved the rare book collections from Sterling Memorial Library to the newly opened Beinecke Rare Book and Manuscript Library and was named Edwin J. Beinecke Research Librarian. A mentor to generations of rare book librarians, she was one of the founders of the Rare Book and Manuscripts Section of the Association of College and Research Libraries of the American Library Association.

Yale University Library Administration

SENIOR LEADERSHIP

Alice Prochaska
University Librarian

Kendall L. Crilly
Associate University Librarian for Program Development and Research

R. Kenny Marone
Associate University Librarian for School and Departmental Libraries and
Director of the Cushing/Whitney Medical Library

Deborah H. McGraw
Associate University Librarian and Chief Administrative Officer

Danuta A. Nitecki
Associate University Librarian for Public Services and Library Teaching and Learning

Ann Shumelda Okerson
Associate University Librarian for Collections and International Programs

Diane Young Turner
Associate University Librarian for Human Resources, Organizational
Development, and Community Relations

Frank M. Turner
John Hay Whitney Professor of History, Associate University Librarian for Special
Collections, and Director of the Beinecke Rare Book and Manuscript Library

ADVISORY COMMITTEE ON LIBRARY POLICY 2009–10

Douglas W. Rae
Chair and Richard S. Ely Professor of Management and Professor of Political Science

Alice Prochaska
University Librarian

Richard Belitsky, M.D.
Deputy Dean for Education, Yale School of Medicine

Meg Bellinger
Director of the Office of Digital Assets and Infrastructure

Hazel V. Carby
Charles C. and Dorathea S. Dilley Professor of African American Studies and Professor of American Studies

Professor Kai Erikson
William R. Kenan, Jr. Professor Emeritus of Sociology and American Studies

Mattie Fitch
Graduate School of Arts and Sciences '14

Basie Bales Gitlin
Yale College '10

Geoffrey Little
Convener and Staff

Philip Long
Chief Information Officer and Director of Information Technology Services

Linda H. Peterson
Niel Gray, Jr. Professor of English

Siobhan Quinlan
Graduate School of Arts and Sciences '13

Holly Rushmeier
Professor of Computer Science

Haun Saussy
Bird White Housum Professor of Comparative Literature and Professor of East Asian Languages and Literatures

J. Lloyd Suttle
Deputy Provost for Academic Resources

Frank M. Turner
John Hay Whitney Professor of History,
Associate University Librarian for Special Collections, and Director of the
Beinecke Rare Book and Manuscript Library

John Harley Warner
Avalon Professor of the History of Medicine and Professor of History and
American Studies

Anders Winroth
Professor of History

Kurt W. Zilm
Professor of Chemistry and Chemical Engineering

YALE LIBRARY ASSOCIATES

OFFICERS
William S. Reese, Chairman
David Alan Richards, Vice Chairman
Frank M. Turner, Secretary
Alice Prochaska, University Librarian

HONORARY COUNCIL MEMBERS
Bromwell Ault
Lawrence G. Blackmon
Ralph W. Franklin
Archibald Hanna
Howard R. Lamar
Richard C. Levin
William P. MacKinnon
Stephen Parks
Joseph W. Reed
Rutherford Rogers
Elihu Rose
William M. Roth

COUNCIL MEMBERS

CLASS OF 2010	CLASS OF 2011
T. Kimball Brooker	Allan E. Bulley III
William N. Goetzmann	Mary Ann Folter
Fred Schreiber	David McCullough
Paul S. Stevens	John R. Robinson
L. Mead Treadwell II	David M. Rumsey
	Robert H. Smith, Jr.

CLASS OF 2012	CLASS OF 2013
J. Weili Cheng	Ronald R. Atkins
Joseph N. Cohen	Hosea Baskin
Andrew P. Davis	Ellen M. Iseman
Lynn Hanke	Frederick R. Koch
John E. Herzog	W. Scott Peterson
A. Tappan Wilder	Emily Rose

UNIVERSITY LIBRARIAN'S DEVELOPMENT COUNCIL

Alice Prochaska, University Librarian
William H. Wright II, Chair

J. Frederick Berg, Jr.
John Robinson Block
Christopher A. di Bonaventura
Barbara E. Franke
Richard J. Franke
Lynn Hanke
Ellen M. Iseman
Erin McBurney
Jerrold Mitchell
William S. Reese
David Alan Richards
Emily Rose
Stephen A. Stack, Jr.
Alan Stamm
Paul S. Stevens